*SISTER*
*TEKESA*
*BLESSING*

# The Seven Keys
# for a Successful
# Apostolic Ministry

By
Alidi Mpateya

*20/9/2014*

**xulon PRESS**

www.xulonpress.com

# Endorsements:

"Dr. Alidi Mpateya in The Seven Keys for a Successful Apostolic Ministry has provided a biblical textbook for Christian leaders in understanding apostolic function, authority and responsibility in the Church today. It is a must read for any serious church leader and lay person who desires to see New Testament power, order and increase in Christ's Body today. Read it. Teach it. Live it!"

**–Dr. Larry Keefauver**
**Bestselling Author, International Teacher**


Revelation of The Seven Keys for a Successful Apostolic Ministryin this book would be of great value to this generation indeed a sound teaching.

**–Pastor Neville Goldman**
**Senior Pastor of Ebenezer Centre,**
**International Teacher.**

# Dedications

This book is dedicated to God, my Lord Jesus Christ, the Holy Ghost, and to all the saints in the kingdom of our Lord and Savior.
Special thanks go to all my sons who worked tirelessly and devoted their time and helped in the typing of the manuscript.

# Table of Contents

# Introduction

# God's Methods Are Timeless

T he church is built upon the foundation of the apostles and prophets. These two ministries are very strategic for the furtherance of the work of God on the earth. The apostolic people of God cannot afford to function outside these two fundamental anointings on which the church is built (Ephesians 2:20). The apostles and prophets give direction and clarity to the church concerning where it should go. However, in this book we will not put an emphasis on the individual anointing of the prophets or apostles. There are many books that have been written that cover those subjects intensely. What we are trying to establish in this book is the overall function of the apostolic people of God.

What I mean by this is the church is first and foremost apostolic. The word apostle means a "sent one." The born again people of God represent Jesus and His church to our world today whether they know it or not. Hence, in this book I am trying to highlight the subject of our apostolic assignment on the earth today. *The Seven Keys for a Successful Apostolic Ministry* will focus on prayer and other activities that relate to our apostolic assignment, and how they became the launching pad for the early church. One of the meanings of the word "reformation" is to "renew." God wants our minds to be renewed or to be changed to an improved state. The way we "do" church, the way we pray, the way we worship, the way we reach out to non-believers, and our general perception on the matters that pertain to our day-to-day lives need to be renewed.

When we look at prayer in the early church we will discover that prayer was one of the most vital tools. The early believers were committed to such a degree of prayer that it was practically impossible for them to do anything without it. Therefore, **prayer** plays a major role for all who want to serve God in our present day. God's methods are timeless. They work all the time. History teaches us that the pioneers of the faith had some major breakthroughs when they employed the particular strategies and methods which I will refer to as the *seven apostolic keys*.

I will be speaking about New Testament **prophecy** and how it relates to us today. I will touch briefly on Old Testament prophecy which functions slightly differently in the New Testament. I would encourage you to read further on this very important subject. I will also highlight and share my thoughts on **evangelism** and **teaching**.

I have dedicated a section dealing with the subject that I call **waiting**. These are days of instant demand where many are not willing to wait for anything. I have discovered that there are even programs on how to become an instant millionaire and all varieties of get rich quick schemes. It is therefore important for those that are of the household of faith to be reminded about waiting or walking in patience before God. Our founding fathers, the heroes of the faith obtained great results through patience and standing in faith.

I also felt it was important to include a study on **unity** because the kingdom of God is a united kingdom. We know God uses the concept of united ruling versus the devil that uses a divide and conquer strategy. **Giving** is a subject near and dear to the Father's heart. As we all know we are a product of the greatest gift God gave to mankind. It took a miracle of God's gift of love to bring us to the loving grace of God. God so loved the world that He gave. You cannot love without giving, but you can give without loving.

I want to encourage you to go into these chapters with a desire to increase your knowledge of each of these important subjects. I pray you will find encouragement, exhortation and comfort. Enjoy the book.

# Chapter One

# Prayer Key

In the fall of 1984, a young man from my neighborhood, Anthony, came and preached the gospel of Jesus Christ to me. At that time being a Rasta was the "in thing." I had friends who were also part of this religion and we were convinced that nothing could be better. As enthusiastic black Africans ignorant of the Truth, we were convinced this religion represented the true Black religion. Most of our time was spent listening to reggae music and reading our "bible." We called these times, "sessions." The sole purpose of these meetings was meditation and getting together. In our sessions we smoked weed as part of our religious practice. We justified this practice by tactfully referring to it as the wisdom weed. This was my life before my conversion.

In my dreadlocks and high on weed, Anthony asked some very pointed questions that really caught my attention: "Do you ever pray? If you do then how and when do you pray?"

These questions made me stop and think. Deep

down I knew that even though I was part of the Rasta religion I had no idea what prayer was. This struck me so hard that I became desperate to know more about prayer. Anthony wasted no time in inviting me to their next midweek Wednesday night service. Wednesday evening came and Anthony came to pick me up just before seven. This was going to be my first time in church as an adult. The last time I remembered attending church was as a young boy, though at the time I had no idea what was going on. Coming from an Islamic background, I was unfamiliar with Sunday school, Bible study or anything Christian. During the midweek service, I noticed almost everyone was praying with such enthusiasm that I was convinced these people knew who they were praying to. The environment was electrifying and exhilarating. I was glad I had accepted the invitation to attend. One thing we never had in our Rastafarian movement was prayer.

This environment was truly different. Before the minister came up to preach I had already made up my mind I wanted to be part of this prayer group. The preacher finished his sermon by inviting those who wanted to give their lives to Christ to come forward. Before he had finished with his invitation I stood up and ran to the front. Since I still had my dreadlocks on, quite a number of people who saw me go up front did not take me seriously. What they didn't realize was that things had already started to change. The minister led us into a sinner's prayer and I gave my life to Christ. This was the first time I ever prayed and it felt great. I could sense I had made a connection with God. I was born again that night. I immediately saw the transforming power of prayer.

## Power of Prayer

This incident gave me an understanding of the power of prayer. Prayer can transform bad character and bad habits into godly ones. It can loosen us from demonic strongholds and produce total freedom even from addictions. As I think about the power of prayer, it reminds me of one of the classic stories in the Bible regarding Samson. After the Philistines had apprehended and incarcerated him in one of their prisons, they plucked out his eyes and kept him bound with chains. As the story goes, they decided to make fun of him as they celebrated before their gods how they had finally apprehended their biggest enemy. It was during this time that Samson asked the young lad that was leading him to show him the pillars of the building.

*And Samson said unto the lad that held him by the hand, Suffer me that I may feel the pillars whereupon the house standeth, that I may lean upon them. Now the house was full of men and women; and all the lords of the Philistines were there; and there were upon the roof about three thousand men and women, that beheld while Samson made sport. And Samson called unto the LORD, and said, O Lord GOD, remember me, I pray thee, and strengthen me, I pray thee, only this once, And Samson took hold of the two middle pillars upon which the house stood, and on which it was borne up, of the one with his right hand, and of the other with his left. O God, that I may be at once avenged of the Philistines for my two eyes. And Samson took hold of the two middle pillars upon which the house stood, and on which it was borne up, of the one with his right hand, and of the other with his left. And Samson said, Let me die with the Philistines. And he bowed himself with all his might; and the house fell upon the lords, and upon all the people that were therein. So the dead which he slew at his death were more than they which he slew in his life. (Judges 16:26-30)*

What a remarkable end! How the power of prayer demolished a building and brought an end to an ungodly celebration party! Greater is the wisdom of God than that of man. What man meant for Samson's harm was turned into a testimony of the power of prayer. When Samson prayed and asked for vengeance over his enemies, God came through in a mighty way.

A similar noteworthy incident is found in the New Testament. Stephen is seen in a posture of prayer regarding those that were persecuting him. Among them was Saul of Tarsus who later became Paul the Apostle.

*Then they cried out with a loud voice, and stopped their ears, and ran upon him with one*

> *accord, And cast him out of the city, and stoned*
> *him: and the witnesses laid down their clothes*
> *at a young man's feet, whose name was Saul.*
> *And they stoned Stephen, calling upon God,*
> *and saying, Lord Jesus, receive my spirit. And*
> *he kneeled down, and cried with a loud voice,*
> *Lord, lay not this sin to their charge. And when*
> *he had said this, he fell asleep. (Acts 7:57-60)*

In the above passage, we see the incident of Stephen after he preached a powerful sermon that provoked the hearts of those that were anti-Christ. They pulled him out of the city, took off his clothes, and laid them at the feet of Saul. While they were busy doing that, Stephen's focus was somewhere totally different. He was calling upon the name of the Lord and saw the Heavens open. While he was going through torture, he knelt down and prayed a prayer of forgiveness for those that were persecuting him. He said, "Lord, lay not this to their charge."

I would like to believe that this is the prayer that led to the conversion of Saul who became Paul the Apostle. The Book of Acts reveals a supernatural encounter that brought this ringleader of those that persecuted Stephen to the point of conversion. This simply shows what God does when we pray.

Jesus spent much of His time in prayer and fasting. I believe that is the reason He was able to overcome most of the challenges of His time. For us to live victoriously it is essential to know how to pray and fast. Prayer must be done on a daily basis. One cannot live without it. Prayer is us saying to God, "We need

You. We can't do without You." As human beings we have limitations, but there is help from above. God is above, we are beneath, and our ways are not His ways. His standards are far greater than ours.

Our Lord Jesus remains the greatest prayer warrior of all time. He is the undisputed master of prayer. He has not resigned. To date He is still holding His championship belt. He continues to be involved in the ministry of prayer as the Scriptures declare, "Wherefore he is able also to save them to the uttermost that come unto God by him, seeing he ever liveth to make intercession for them" (Hebrews 7:25). This verse speaks of Jesus interceding for the saints. He is the go-between for us. He stands in the gap on behalf of man to God. As the scripture has said, "He lives forever to intercede with God on their behalf" (NLT).

Jesus lived such a life of prayer that His disciples asked Him, to teach them to pray. "And it came to pass, that, as he was praying in a certain place, when he ceased, one of his disciples said unto him, Lord, teach us to pray, as John also taught his disciples" (Luke 11:1). I am convinced that everything Jesus did was a direct result of prayer. All the miracles He performed were linked to His prayer life. Our Lord Jesus is now seated at the right hand of God and continues to intercede for us. "Who is even at the right hand of God, who also maketh intercession for us" (Romans 8:34).

Jesus is our mediator in the new covenant; the high priest of our confession, "Wherefore, holy brethren, partakers of the heavenly calling, consider the Apostle and High Priest of our profession, Christ Jesus"

(Hebrews 3:1). The Old Testament prophet Isaiah confirms this by saying, "He was numbered with the transgressors; and he bare the sin of many, and made intercession for the transgressors" (Isaiah 53:12).

Right from the beginning, Jesus' earthly ministry was characterized by intense prayer and guidance from the Holy Spirit. "Then was Jesus led up of the Spirit into the wilderness to be tempted of the devil" (Matthew 4:1). In this scripture we see Jesus being led into the wilderness where He fasted for forty days and nights then He was tempted by the devil. Here is an example of spiritual warfare where Jesus did not take Himself into the battle arena, the Spirit of God led Him there. This is a level of prayer that brings us into direct confrontation with the devil. In this level it is the Spirit of God that will be fighting through us. Scripture says we should not be worried even if we are brought before the judges for the Spirit of God will speak on our behalf (see Mark 13:11).

## Standing in the Gap Through Intercession

*Even them will I bring to my holy mountain, and make them joyful in my house of prayer: their burnt offerings and their sacrifices shall be accepted upon mine altar; for mine house shall be called a house of prayer for all people. (Isaiah 56:7)*

The church is where the Spirit of God resides. It's more than a building, it's a community that represents the power of God. The Apostle Paul writes

to Timothy, his spiritual son saying, "I exhort therefore, that, first of all, supplications, prayers, inter-
cessions, and giving of thanks, be made for all men"
(1 Timothy 2:1). Paul said these words under the
influence of the Holy Ghost. His key words were,
"first of all," meaning something that comes first
in order or rank. In other words Paul was saying
prayer must be our first priority.

He went on to break it down and mentioned
intercession. Let us look at the word intercession.
*Intercession* simply means standing in the gap
for others or pleading to God on behalf of others.
Prayer is one of the subjects Apostles are required
to know about and do. "Pray without ceasing. Pray
at all times" (1 Thessalonians 5:17).

Prayer is an important aspect that seems to be
ignored in the modern day church. Christians today
seem to have a very casual approach when it comes
to the subject of prayer. The early church was not
so. Its foundation was laid on prayer. The disciples
had such a desire to learn about prayer that they
asked Jesus to teach them to pray. Therefore prayer
must be the most desired and sought after element
in the life of every child of God. Prayer is the only
channel that connects us to our Heavenly Father.
Destinies are defined through this channel and
divine strategies are unraveled in prayer.

The present day apostolic reformation needs
greater information on this subject of prayer.
Remember that the first church was founded upon
a prayer movement that was conducted in the upper
room with approximately 120 people. For ten days

they prayed continuously and a revival was birthed.

Jesus told His disciples, "The harvest truly is great, but the labourers are few: pray ye therefore the Lord of the harvest, that he would send forth labourers into his harvest" (Luke 10:2).

Our Lord said the harvest is plenty but the labourers are few and He went on to say, "Ask the Lord of the harvest, therefore, to send out workers into his harvest field" (NIV). The word "ask" means to make a request for something. It is synonymous with the word prayer. Without asking or praying, there will be no harvest. In other words the salvation of the nations and of our loved ones is dependent on our prayers. In Psalm 2:8 the Lord said, "Ask of Me, and I will give You the nations for Your inheritance"(NKJV).

We live in the day and age where the church's effectiveness is measured by its ability to advertise itself. We advertise through billboards, electronic media, newsletters, and infomercials. Churches are advertised more than Coca-Cola advertises its products. There is nothing wrong with advertising, but prayer produces more results. The word of the Lord from the Book of Psalms says,

"Ask of me, and I shall give thee the heathen for thine inheritance, and the uttermost parts of the earth for thy possession" (Psalm 2:8). The Lord never said advertise, He said ask Him for nations. Therefore our cry should be, "God give us the nations." We should not be obsessed or preoccupied with power seeking, or be caught up in debates which seek to prove who is chief among us. There are some apostolic networks today that claim to be favourites of God. I've heard some even say, "Let there be regulation of preachers who come to preach in our cities." They believe in screening preachers before they are allowed to minister to any church in their area.

This is a matter of concern and the question should be asked whose methods are at play in this regard. No one is called to be God's policeman. Prayer is the only weapon that can expose the devil's advocates. By simply reading the Acts of the Apostles, you will discover that the Spirit of God exposed all gainsayers and soothsayers such as the sons of Sceva, Ananias and Sapphira, and Simon the sorcerer. These are some of the biblical examples of people whose missions were exposed by the Holy Spirit. It does not matter what positions we hold; we cannot fight for God. Some so called apostolic networks are nothing but a stumbling block in the kingdom of God. I have heard titles like the Apostle of Africa, the Apostle of the Continent, or the Apostle of the Hour; all these titles mean nothing. Who shall pray and cry for the souls that they may not perish? God is looking for a people that stand in prayer and that ask the Lord of the Harvest for labourers.

The modern day church has been caught up in vain debates over unnecessary issues. For example, some apostolic movements are preaching messages such as; the casting out of the devils is outdated; fasting and praying is not for our day; and you don't have to lay hands on anyone. Some say healing is for today some say it's not. Some are seeking to vote others into power. Some say we must wait for another and seek the most connected Apostle. The Word of God clearly says that the world is waiting for the manifestation of the sons of God. We need to be among those who seek nothing but the harvest of souls. These are the kingdom demonstrators that turn the world upside down for the Lord Jesus Christ. It is about time that we begin to pray against the spirit of denominationalism, individualism, racism, and xenophobia in our present day apostolic reformation, and ask God for the harvest of nations.

## Prayer Changes Things

The city of Ninevah was doomed for destruction. God, through the mouth of Jonah, brought a message of judgment that the city was to be destroyed. "And Jonah began to enter into the city a day's journey, and he cried, and said, Yet forty days, and Nineveh shall be overthrown" (Jonah 3:4). However, the city responded in sincerity and proclaimed a solemn fast, whereby they called everybody to join in; including the suckling babies. They extended this fast to include their animals as well. They were so remorseful as they came before God in prayer that God hearkened unto their prayer and saved the entire nation.

*So the people of Nineveh believed God, and proclaimed a fast, and put on sackcloth, from the greatest of them even to the least of them. (Jonah 3:3) But let man and beast be covered with sackcloth, and cry mightily unto God: yea, let them turn everyone from*

*his evil way, and from the violence that is in
their hands. Who can tell if God will turn and
repent, and turn away from his fierce anger,
that we perish not? And God saw their works,
that they turned from their evil way; and God
repented of the evil, that he had said that he
would do unto them; and he did it not. (Jonah
3:8-10)*

Once again we see how prayer saved a nation
from perishing. When people believe God and cry
out to Him for His mercy, it is possible to bring an
entire nation into the kingdom of God.

There is another example in the Book of Esther
where a person who had a vendetta against Esther's
people conspired against them. He brought a false
accusation to the king, implying they were not
law-abiding and did not submit to the rules of the
Kingdom. He even offered to carry out a massacre
of these people by incurring the costs upon himself
to make sure they would not exist in the kingdom. It
was during that time that Esther became aware of the
plot and responded prayerfully saying, "Go, gather
together all the Jews that are present in Shushan,
and fast ye for me, and neither eat nor drink three
days, night or day: I also and my maidens will fast
likewise; and so will I go in unto the king, which is
not according to the law: and if I perish, I perish"
(Esther 4:16).

Esther decreed fasting and prayer as preparation before confronting the king, even though it was
risky. She even mentioned that the king could have

her executed, but in order for her to carry her plan out successfully, she needed the divine intervention of God's hand. So prayer was the only means that was available to bring about change. One thing we need to note is that a verdict had already been passed by the king, and a date had already been allocated for the extermination of the Jewish nation to be carried-out. "And the king took his ring from his hand, and gave it unto Haman the son of Hammedatha the Agagite, the Jews' enemy. And the king said unto Haman, The silver is given to thee, the people also, to do with them as it seemeth good to thee"(Esther 3:10-11).

It is interesting to know what prayer can do. Throughout the Bible, there are many examples we can learn and draw encouragement from. It doesn't matter what kind of difficult situation we find ourselves in. There is power that can turn events around. When we call out to God in prayer, believing sincerely that He is our Heavenly Father and that His plans are not for doom but for good, we will triumph over our enemies (see Jeremiah 29:11). We are the sheep of His pasture and He is our good shepherd. He can take us from a zero to hero, from gloom to glory, and from test to testimony no matter what the situation may appear to be. The story of Esther has a dramatic end and displays how the power of prayer works. The evil that was meant for Esther's people was reversed and placed on the very person who conspired against them. He ended up drinking his own poison. What a mighty God we serve.

The prayers that Esther offered created an

opportunity for her to go and present her case before the king, even though it was against the odds. To come before the king required a certain procedure. However in her case, prayer made an opening for Esther and she received favor in her presentation before the king. Prayer can create a platform of favor as seen in Esther's case.

> *Then Esther the queen answered and said, "If I have found favour in thy sight, O king, and if it please the king, let my life be given me at my petition, and my people at my request." (Esther 7:3) Then the king Ahasuerus answered and said unto Esther the queen, "Who is he, and where is he, that durst presume in his heart to do so?"(Esther 7:5) And Harbonah, one of the chamberlains, said before the king, "Behold also, the gallows fifty cubits high, which Haman had made for Mordecai, who had spoken good for the king, standeth in the house of Haman." Then the king said, "Hang him thereon." So they hanged Haman on the gallows that he had prepared for Mordecai. Then was the king's wrath pacified. (Esther 7:9-10)*

In the above Scriptures we see how the power of prayer released God to intervene in a tremendous way. We see Esther's enemy hanged at the very place that he wanted Modercai, Esther's uncle to hang.

## Prayer Empowers the Preaching of the Gospel

*Finally, brethren, pray for us, that the word of the Lord may have free course, and be glorified, even as it is with you." (2 Thessalonians 3:1)*

The Apostle Paul pleaded with the church community for prayer. His request was specific; pray so that the gospel may spread. Paul knew that with the support of prayer the gospel would have inroads and would reach desired destinies. The kingdom of darkness tries to hinder the spread of the gospel by all conceivable means, therefore the Apostle Paul requested the saints at Thessalonica to pray; knowing the power of corporate prayer.

When closely studying the history of the New Testament Church, we discover that the foundation of the early church was prayer. Without prayer it would have been impossible for the early church to have the impact and the breakthroughs it had, and become the incubator of Evangelism that it was. Prayer was one of the most powerful tools the early church possessed. This praying made the early church a spiritual power house. Prayer is a broad and multi-dimensional subject. We want to try and explore some of these dimensions further, while avoiding anything that will generalize and put prayer in a box.

## The Dimensions of Prayer

We want to be careful not to miss out on the

blessings that prayer releases. During His days of earthly ministry, our Lord Jesus Christ demonstrated many dimensions of prayer that provide us with teachings we can all learn from. He revealed some key strategies on how we ought to use the kind of prayer that removes obstacles from our lives. Sometimes we pray and don't get results because we pray amiss.

*Ye ask, and receive not, because ye ask amiss, that ye may consume it upon your lusts. (James 4:3)*

It is important to note that our prayers should not be offered to God in order for them to please our flesh and lustful desires. We should be specific when praying. Jesus left us an example of how every human being must pray.

*Who in the days of his flesh, when he had offered up prayers and supplication, strong crying and tears unto him that was able to save him from death and was heard in that he feared. (Hebrews 5:7)*

Listed below are four dimensions we need to pay attention to: prayers, supplication, strong cries and Godly fear.

## 1. Prayers

Prayer simply means asking or making requests.

It is communication with God in an effort to receive the supernatural intervention of God's hand in our situations. We can do this in various ways, one of which is through an *all-night prayer session* as seen in the passages below.

*And he went a little further, and fell on his face, and prayed, saying, O my Father, if it be possible, let this cup pass from me: nevertheless not as I will, but as thou wilt. (Matthew 26:39)*

*And it came to pass in those days, that he went out into a mountain to pray, and continued all night in prayer to God.* (Luke 6:12)

On the night of His betrayal, Jesus continued all night in prayer and sought strength from God. He needed strength to allow the will of God to surpass His. He yielded to the will of God because His death was to give life to many. All night prayer releases apostolic strategies. They are very effective, as seen in the Book of Acts. After Peter had been thrown into prison the Bible says the church prayed all night for him. The angels visited Peter that very night and released him from prison (Acts 12:1-17). All night prayer held on behalf of Peter released the heavenly host to minister. Prayer releases angelic ministry. In another incident, at midnight Paul and Silas sang praises to God and the prison doors were opened (Acts 16:23-34). I have personally witnessed the power of all night prayer. When the church spends time in prayer, the power of God is released in an unprecedented way; affecting every region and local church.

Fasting combined with prayer often usher us into this realm. Fasting is an offensive weapon that gives us power in the spirit realm. It gives us the same spiritual perception that enabled Jesus to overcome every temptation the devil cast at Him. His victory was also celebrated by the heavenly angels that came down and ministered to Him. When we fast and pray we engage in warfare against the enemy and his forces. Victory is assured for the child of God.

*And when he had fasted forty days and forty nights, he was afterward hungered. (Matthew 4:2)*

*Then the devil leaveth him, and, behold, angels came and ministered unto him. (Matthew 4:11)*

When we fast and pray, we overcome the devil and the angels of the Lord will minister to us. True prayer dethrones the devil and releases the heavenly host. Jesus knew that prayer was the key to the establishment of the kingdom of God on the earth. If we are prayerful, we frustrate the devil and play a part in the expansion of the influence the kingdom of God has on earth.

Even our Lord Jesus Christ invested a substantial amount of time in prayers for the universal church. I believe the Body of Christ was birthed by the prayers of our Lord and Savior Jesus Christ. The unity we enjoy, the faith we confess, and the common doctrine that binds us are all a result of the prayers that were offered to God. Our continuity and our establishment in the fundamental teachings of our Lord and Savior are directly linked to His prayers. In John 17:9, Jesus prayed for the church and for those who were to believe on His name through the preaching of the gospel. "I pray for them: I pray not for the world, but for them which thou hast given me; for they are thine."

His prayer was specific. He knew all that were His. Everything that God gives us can only be preserved through prayer. Everything that we have received is sustained in God. Our lives, our families, and the friendships we share cannot be fruitful without God. Jesus prayed that none of us would fail.

The apostle Paul writes, "Who shall separate us from the love of Christ? Shall tribulation, or distress, or persecution, or famine, or nakedness, or peril, or sword? (Romans 8:35). I believe that Paul was writing in reference to the prayers of our Lord Jesus. He had a deep conviction and understanding that what Jesus had prayed for would stand forever.

Jesus, in His own words, said as He prayed, "Father, I thank you that you have heard me. I knew that you always hear me" (John 11:41-42 NIV). When Jesus prayed, He moved the hand of God. Evidently diseases and sicknesses could not stand when He prayed. He released the healing hand of God through His prayers. These are some of the many reasons why we should pray. The Bible says,

"Is any sick among you? Let him call the elders of the church...And the prayer of faith shall save the sick" (James 5:14-15). Our Lord Jesus did not pray for just one aspect of our lives, but covered all areas of a believer's life. Prayer is beyond any technology and what money can buy. Jesus healed the sick by the power of God.

A friend of mine once asked me to pray for his sister who was in a critical condition. I prayed for her and told her that she would sleep like a baby that very night. The following morning my phone rang and it was her, she had been healed that night. She was so excited that she brought her family members to see me. They were keen to know what had brought such a tremendous change! I used the opportunity to preach Jesus to them. The whole family received Christ that day and renounced Buddhism entirely. Her miracle brought salvation to the whole family. The Bible declares in Acts 10:38, "How God anointed Jesus of Nazareth with the Holy Ghost and with power: who went about doing good, and healing all that were oppressed of the devil; for God was with him."

There is no occasion or situation in our lives that should not be prayed for. When planning for celebrations and anniversaries, prayer is important. Prayer shields us from the eleventh hour disappointments. We pray not only because we are financially strained, we pray to avoid the disappointments and eleventh hour emergencies, such as the unexpected crowds' even guests with huge appetites. Prayer is the only antidote. Jesus' mother understood the importance of prayer in celebrations; hence she asked Jesus for a miracle at the wedding at Cana (John 2:1-10).

Furthermore our Lord prayed for sinners. When the Pharisees brought a woman that had been caught in act of adultery, Jesus interceded for her by challenging the self-righteous crowd saying that whoever had no sin should throw the first stone (John 8:3-11). When we pray and confess our sins God forgives us. Prayer is a total dependence on God. When it simply means we are admitting to God we are not able to do things on our own.

In the Lord's Prayer, Jesus taught us that we should forgive when we pray (Matthew 6:12). To forgive when we pray means we understand that we coexist with imperfect people. Therefore, if our fellow man transgresses, we should find time to present them to God in prayer. Jesus forgave in the most difficult of situations. When He had been apprehended and men gave false witness against Him; He forgave. Even when He hung on the cross, Jesus forgave those who had done this to Him. This serves as an example for us that we do not have to forgive only when things are going our way, but we should walk in forgiveness. True forgiveness is letting go when it is most difficult.

In 2 Peter 2:5, the Apostle Peter highlights the fact that every believer is a priest in the house of God. The church is a representative of the priestly function of Jesus Christ. When the people of God begin to operate in their priestly anointing the church will move out of its comfort zone, and will perform service unto God. God in turn often manifests the glory of His presence. Without fulfilling our priestly duties by offering the sacrifice of prayer and offerings unto God, the suffering of God's people will increase. Disease, famine, and all the ills of the world will continue to cripple mankind. If the people that are called by God's name neglect their duties of prayer, the world cannot be changed.

History teaches us that God worked hand in hand with men and women of prayer, to bring about change and revival. God is looking for men and women who will stand in the gap for the hurting people of this world.

*If my people, which are called by my name, shall humble themselves, and pray, and seek my face, and turn from their wicked ways; then will I hear from heaven, and will forgive their sin and will heal their land. (2 Chronicles 7:14)*

Prayers should be made for the saints. The Apostle James made a powerful observation regarding the subject of prayer. Historians maintain that James was a man of prayer. There is a belief or a saying that the skin on his knees was thick beyond natural thickness due to the amount of time he spent kneeling in prayer. We may not be able to substantiate that as fact, however he had this to say regarding prayer.

*Confess your faults one to another, and pray one for another, that ye may be healed. The effectual fervent prayer of a righteous man availeth much.* (James 5:16)

Fervent means showing ardent or extremely passionate enthusiasm. It also means glowing as a result of intense heat. Jesus prayed in the garden of Gethsemane until His sweat dripped as drops of blood. Would it be possible that His passion was glowing out or shall we say He had the burning passion to fulfill His mission on earth? What do you think would happen if the church began to burn with passion? If the fervent prayer of the righteous has impact, then assuredly God will move on our behalf. Prayers that bring transformation are prayers of the righteous; not the famous head of states, celebrities, kings, or politicians of this world. God is not moved by our occupations in the world. Kings and politicians of this world do not move the hand of God, but it is the prayer of the righteous that brings God into the affairs of mankind.

Prayer books and religious methods carry no value. Righteous means to be in right standing with God. It is those that are in right standing with God that bring about transformation.

*Blessed is the nation whose God is the LORD; and the people whom he hath chosen for his own inheritance.* (Psalm 33:12)

Therefore prayer must be pivotal to the success of our schools and our public institutions. It is through more prayer that a nation is empowered. Through prayer, a nation is secure. The question then that we must ask is: "Will the size of our army and the number of our nuclear weapons build our nation?" The answer is of course, "No!" It is the fervent prayer of the righteous that avails much. As the scripture says, "What shall we then say to these things? If God be for us, who can be against us?" (Romans 8:31).

Nations should not put their trust in their defense forces, regardless of how good they are. Man-made weapons are limited compared to the power of prayer. "Some trust in chariots, and some in horses: but we will remember the name of the LORD our God" (Psalm 20:7).

The declaration of our trust in God must not only be a matter of empty words or billboards that we put up. The true confession of our faith must be based on our prayers. Even when we go through trials our focus should be on God. Emotions don't resolve any-thing. We should take all our burdens to the Lord in prayer.

## 2. Supplication

Supplication means an appeal made to someone in authority or a humble and sincere request to someone who has the power to grant that request. Prayers of supplication are, therefore, detailed appeals that we present to God so that He may grant us our requests. Sometimes this may entail writing down our petitions and bringing them before God, like someone going to the high court to speak to a judge. There was an occasion in the Old Testament where King Hezekiah received a threatening letter from Rabshakeh, King of Ethiopia which he took and presented to God, desiring the intervention of God.

*And Hezekiah received the letter from the hand of the messengers, and read it: and Hezekiah went up unto the house of the LORD, and spread it before the LORD. And Hezekiah prayed unto the LORD, saying, O LORD of hosts, God of Israel, that dwellest between the cherubims, thou art the God, even thou alone, of all the kingdoms of the earth: thou hast made heaven and earth. (Isaiah 37:14-16) Supplication is a kind of prayer that requires sincerity and humility. It is important to note that prayer and humility are intertwined. And the king said again unto Esther on the second day at the banquet of wine, What is thy petition, Queen Esther? And it shall bè granted thee: and what is thy request? And it shall be performed, even to the half of the kingdom. (Esther 7:2)*

Esther was a humble woman of prayer. In the above scripture, the king was responding to her petition. He wanted specific details on what she required so that it could be performed for her, even if it meant giving her half of the kingdom. The lesson we learn from that is humility and sincerity release that which is beyond our expectation. A humble and contrite heart, that is not puffed up will position us in a place of receiving. Hence, we have the words of our Lord

Jesus Christ in one of His lessons on prayer.

> *And when thou prayest, thou shalt not be*
> *as the hypocrites are: for they love to pray*
> *standing in the synagogues and in the cor-*
> *ners of the streets, that they may be seen of*
> *men. Verily I say unto you, they have their*
> *reward. (Matthew 6:5)*

God hears us even if we don't make a lot of noise.
There are some nationalities which believe if you are
not screaming, you are not making any contact with
God. I wonder if that is true? We get a good example
in the case of Hannah in 1 Samuel 1:14 who did not
shout aloud but got God's attention. Supplication is
not in the tone of voice. Rather it is a humble and
sincere spirit that seeks to present a case to the high
court in heaven and to our Father God, with an assurance that He will come through and fight for us.

In the garden of Gethsemane Jesus reasoned
with God and thereafter found the strength to face
His prosecutors (Matthew 26:42). Peter, on the other
hand, had yet to grasp the power of prayer. When
the Roman soldiers came to arrest Jesus he engaged
in a physical fight. He drew his sword and cut off a
soldier's ear, only to have Jesus restore the ear (Luke
22:49-51). One thing we have to remember, our
fight is in the spiritual world and not in the physical
world (Ephesians 6:12). When we are without prayer
there is the likelihood that we may find ourselves
responding naturally instead of spiritually.

Jesus based His reaction on the understanding

that since He had already made a petition to God and He knew His Father was going to rise up and fight for Him. He surrendered to the will of God. It's quite easy to think that we can use our own strength to fight our battles if we are not a praying people. It is essential to learn to offer detailed supplication to God.

> *Then Simon Peter having a sword drew it, and smote the high priest's servant, and cut off his right ear. The servant's name was Malchus. (John 18:10)*

### 3. Strong Cries

Another dimension that we need to pay attention to is "strong cries." Crying is often associated with weakness, infancy, fear or lack of confidence. I want to use an example that I picked up during the time I was ministering among people of Asian descent. I gave my personal testimony and began to cry in the middle of the sermon, overwhelmed by how much God had transformed my life. Among some of the Asian culture it's unfamiliar and unacceptable for a man to cry in front of people. Even the pastor of that church felt I had embarrassed myself and should not have cried. To them it was a sign of weakness. I felt bad after discovering that, but comforted myself thereafter knowing Jesus had done something similar. The shortest verse in the Bible is in reference to when Jesus cried (John 11:35). There is also another place in the Bible that speaks of our Lord Jesus Christ crying. "And when he was come near, he beheld the city, and wept over it," (Luke 19:41).

When people refer to crying as being childlike, I agree in one regard, basing this on the words of our Master when He said we should receive the kingdom of God as a child. "Verily I say unto you, whosoever shall not receive the kingdom of God as a little child, he shall not enter therein" (Mark 10:15).

In the kingdom of God, we need to be like children in order for us to reach the levels that God has called us for. If I cry as a child to my Heavenly Father it shows my total dependency on Him, knowing that He will come through for me. Our God hears our cries and attends to every petition. Hence Jesus said, "In this manner, therefore pray: Our Father in heaven..." (Matthew 6:9). When we cry as God's children, we are not being cowardly; we are simply seeking our Father's attention and assistance.

When God appeared to Moses in Exodus 3:9 He said, "Now therefore, behold, the cry of the children of Israel is come unto me: and I have also seen the oppression wherewith the Egyptians oppress them." I often ask myself if the children of Israel had not cried out would God have come through for them? God responded to their cry for help and sent them a deliverer. We should not overlook the power of crying. The children of Israel did not just cry out for nothing, they cried because of the oppression of the Egyptians.

Crying reminds me of a certain preacher who loved saying, "If nothing else works, try crying." In the days of His flesh, our Lord Jesus offered up strong cries and tears unto God. When Lazarus died, Jesus wept, and God heard Him. David the King also had the habit of crying before God. He shares an interesting fact about God and our tears in Psalm 56:8. "Thou tellest my wanderings: put thou my tears into thy bottle: are they not in thy book?" When we cry to God it is not in vain, our tears are recorded in heaven.

Revelation 7:17 says, "For the Lamb which is in the midst of the throne shall feed them, and shall lead them unto living fountains of waters: and God shall wipe away all tears from their eyes." How could God wipe our tears away if we never cried? The psalmist said, "They that sow in tears shall reap in joy" (Psalm 126:5).

The Bible is full of examples of people who cried before God. There is Hezekiah who was in need of more time and cried unto the Lord. God told the prophet to, "Go, and say to Hezekiah, 'Thus saith the LORD, the God of David thy father, I have heard thy prayer, I have seen thy tears: behold, I will add unto thy days fifteen years' " (Isaiah 38:5). Job, in his affliction said, "My friends scorn me: but mine eye poureth out tears unto God" (Job 16:20).

The Apostle Paul wrote to the church at Corinth out of concern for the state the church was in saying, "For out of much affliction and anguish of heart I wrote unto you with many tears; not that ye should be grieved, but that ye might know the love which I have more abundantly unto you" (2 Corinthians 2:4). The Apostle Paul had a burden for the church at Corinth and desired to see them walk in the ways of God. This church was very zealous, but lacked knowledge. As Paul' letters were written with tears caused by their lack of guidance and stability.

*"Therefore watch, and remember, that by the space of three years I ceased not to warn every one night and day with tears." (Acts 20:31)*

### 4. Godly Fear

*Who in the days of his flesh, when he had offered up prayers and supplications with strong crying and tears unto him that was able to save him from death, and was heard in that he feared. (Hebrews 5:7)*

Jesus offered strong cries and tears to God showing how sincere we ought to be in our prayers and supplications. He prayed to be saved from death; He "was heard in that he feared." The Amplified translation of this verse gives us further insight as to what this verse truly means. "In the days of His flesh [Jesus] offered up definite, special petitions [for that which He not only wanted but needed] and **supplications with strong crying and tears** to Him Who was [always] able to save Him [out] from death, and He was heard because of His reverence toward God [**His godly fear**, His piety, in that He shrank from the horrors of separation from the bright presence of the Father]" (emphasis added).

The Bible says, "The fear of God is the beginning of wisdom: and the knowledge of the holy is understanding" Proverbs 9:10). Everyone who has a successful relationship with God possesses some level of Godly fear. The fear of God is shed upon our hearts by the Holy Spirit; it is the kind of fear that does not seek to enslave us, scare us, or horrifies us, but liberates us to walk in the commandments of God. "Behold, the eye of the LORD is upon them that fear him, upon them that hope in his mercy" (Psalm 33:18).

When men walk in the reverential fear of God there is absolutely nothing God will withhold from them. It is seen from the account when God wanted to destroy Sodom and Gomorrah, but would not do so without revealing it to Abraham. In Genesis 18:20, the LORD said to Abraham, "Because the cry of Sodom and Gomorrah is great, and because their sin is very grievous."

God-fearing people possess the ability to negotiate with God, for the saving of a nation. The reason God wanted to destroy Sodom and Gomorrah was due to their great sin which had come before God. Hence, God was preparing to unleash judgment, but note the relationship Abraham had with God. It put him in a place to negotiate with God for the salvation of that nation. Read this amazing conversation between God and Abraham that we have the privilege to sit in on.

> *Peradventure there be fifty righteous within the city: wilt thou also destroy and not spare the place for the fifty righteous that are therein? That be far from thee to do after this manner, to slay the righteous with the wicked: and that the righteous should be as the wicked, that be far from thee: Shall not the Judge of all the earth*

> *do right? And he said unto him, Oh let not the*
> *Lord be angry, and I will speak: Peradventure*
> *there shall thirty be found there. And he said,*
> *I will not do it, if I find thirty there. (Genesis*
> *18:24, 25, 30)*

God-fearing people in our communities are very important. Their fear of God is useful when it comes to intercession, for it possesses the ability for them to negotiate with God on behalf of their communities. In the case of Abraham regarding Sodom, we see him shifting as he spoke to God asking him if different numbers of people were present would God change His mind. The ability to negotiate speaks of the level of relationship Abraham had with God. That relationship came from his walk of reverential fear of God. There is a level of faith that God fearing people operate in. They have a confidence in God that even when they have not asked for anything, God gives.

At the beginning of this dimension of prayer, we mentioned Godly fear and used Hebrews 5:7 as it speaks of Jesus being heard for the reason that He feared God. I want to challenge you! Do you fear God? The fear of God channels us in the route of answered prayers. The Old Testament provides us with a classic example of a group of women who feared God. Pharaoh wanted all male children born of Hebrew women killed, but because these midwives feared God they saved the lives of these male children. The fear of God gave the midwives wisdom to preserve the lives of innocent children.

> *But the midwives feared God, and did not as the king of Egypt commanded them, but saved the men children alive. And the king of Egypt called for the midwives, and said unto them, Why have ye done this thing, and have saved the men children alive? And the midwives said unto Pharaoh, because the Hebrew women are not as the Egyptian women; for they are lively, and are delivered ere the midwives come in unto them. Therefore God dealt well with the midwives: and the people multiplied, and waxed very mighty. And it came to pass, because the midwives feared God, that he made them houses. (Exodus 1:17-21)*

This passage teaches us an important lesson that must be learned. The God-fearing midwives are said to have received houses from God. It is important to note that prosperity, houses and land come from God. At times it may also mean promoting or blessing His people that walk in His ways and abstain from evil, such as the ones referred to in the above text. This act of killing male children at birth was indeed an evil act. It is not so different however from those that practice abortion. Abortion is still the killing of children. No one is to kill an unborn child for whatever reason. Sometimes poverty is directly linked to our disobedience.

Children are a gift from God. Mothers need to know that children have a destiny and their lives began at conception. The fear of God in the midwives preserved Moses. The children of Israel would not have known Moses the great deliverer if there had been no God-fearing midwives.

> *Before I formed thee in the belly I knew thee; and before thou camest forth out of the womb I sanctified thee, and I ordained thee a prophet unto the nations. (Jeremiah 1:5)*

The story of the four Jewish boys in Babylon is another good example of God-fearing people. God gave them favor in everything they did, because they purposed in their hearts that they would not defile themselves with the portions of the King.

> *But Daniel purposed in his heart that he would not defile himself with the portion of the king's meat, nor with the wine which he drank: therefore he requested of the prince of the eunuchs that he might not defile himself. (Daniel 1:8)*

The four boys in Babylon found themselves in a situation similar to that of the midwives; they went against the decree of the King in order to stay true to God. They did not touch any defilement on the king's table; the midwives on the other hand would not defile themselves by the decree of the king who wanted them to kill children at birth. Godly fear is very practical; it puts value on what God values.

Here is another scenario showing us the power of reverential fear. On the day Jesus was crucified, two thieves were crucified with Him. They were in a conversation with each other as they hung on their crosses as seen in Luke 23:40, "But the other answering rebuked him, saying, 'Dost not thou fear God, seeing thou art in the same condemnation?'" It was the fear of God that gave this condemned individual the ability to recognize the Son of God, and wisdom to speak carefully about Him. Therefore he was assured a place in paradise. One would say the fear of God gives birth to revelation, and revelation takes you to the next level. In this example there was an instant elevation due to Godly fear. God expects us to do His will to show that we fear Him.

# Chapter Two

# Waiting Is the Key

There is a saying used in Christian circles commonly referred to as "quiet time." This is designated quality time one dedicates to God at the beginning of each day to fellowship and meditate on His Word. It is in these times that God gives nuggets of revelation that equip individuals with the ability to carry out day-to-day programs with an assurance of God's divine assistance. This quiet time can be traced back to the days of Jesus, as this was His custom. He would withdraw Himself from all His disciples and the crowds to spend quality time with His Father in meditation. Quality time with God produces dynamic power to perform the unusual. No wonder at one stage Jesus walked on the surface of the water (see Matthew 14:25-33). In this chapter I want to shed more light on the importance of quiet time giving emphasis on its most basic quality, "waiting."

*And, being assembled together with them,*
*commanded them that they should not depart*

*from Jerusalem, but **wait** for the promise of
the Father, which, saith he, ye have heard of
me. (Acts 1:4 emphasis added)*

It was Jesus who pioneered and developed the art
of waiting. In His earthly ministry He waited upon
God and taught His apostles to do it as well. It was
a golden strategy to be passed on to all generations.
Today no one is willing to wait. We are all go-get-
ters, and we get what we want now, even if it is at
someone else's expense. However, in the kingdom
of God the will of God supersedes the will of man.
It is best to desire God's will for your life, even if it
means waiting.

Satan's philosophy is contradictory; it says, "Get
it any how!" This was illustrated in the biblical story
of Adam where the devil used deception to steal
Adam's dominion, which has detrimentally affected
the entire universe.

With our focus on waiting, let's take a look at
some of the examples our Lord Jesus Christ taught
and lived. He was practical in His teachings. He also
expects us to not only do as He said, but do even
more than He did. He walked His talk with authen-
ticity and selflessness, not as a hypocrite.

Jesus pioneered the walk of our faith; He is the
Chief in command and the Apostle of our confession. The following statement is true and worthy of
serious consideration. "Wherefore, holy brethren,
partakers of the heavenly calling, consider the
Apostle and High Priest of our profession, Christ
Jesus" (Hebrews 3:1).

## Wait for God's Perfect Timing

Before His ascension to heaven, Jesus commanded His disciples to learn to wait upon the Lord. I personally believe that this was the most important instruction ever given to them. A close study of the word "command" shows it is an order or instruction given by somebody in authority. The command given to the disciples was that they must wait for the power from above. As the Chief in command Jesus was watchful not to deploy them without a mandate, proper authority, and power for their assignment. "… but wait for the promise of the Father, which, saith he, ye have heard of me" (Acts 1:4).

He said that they were to become witnesses. This commandment should be a universal kingdom mandate to every believer. Every disciple and every apostle desiring to do the work of ministry as commanded by our Lord Jesus Christ should have patience as a virtue.

By instructing them to wait, Jesus gave them one of the fundamental keys He Himself used for a success in ministry. It is important not to re-invent the wheel, but to embrace winning formulas developed by former pioneers. Jesus gave them the universal and eternal principles that He had applied and which had prospered His ministry. He was the kind of leader that set the pace for His followers.

*The thing that hath been, it is that which shall be; and that which is done is that which shall be done: and there is no new thing under the sun." (Ecclesiastes 1:9) To everything there is a season, and a time to every purpose under the heaven." (Ecclesiastes 3:1)*

Solomon confirms the fact that there is nothing new under the sun. Even the devil is not an unknown super power emerging from obscurity to scare people or challenge God. He was defeated at the cross through the death and resurrection of our Lord Jesus Christ. He is still defeated to this day by the saints who call upon the name of the Lord.

If he is the same old devil who was defeated then, can he not be defeated now? History tells us, "Those who cannot remember the past are condemned to repeat it." The Bible says it this way, "Thus saith the LORD, Stand ye in the ways, and see, and ask for the old paths, where is the good way, and walk therein, and ye shall find rest for your souls. But they said, we will not walk therein" (Jeremiah 6:16).

A good example of learning from the past is taken from the story of King David. On the day he was about to defeat Goliath the giant, young David spoke with King Saul, regarding using the King's armor in battle. "And David girded his sword upon his armour, and he assayed to go; for he had not proved it. And David said unto Saul, 'I cannot go with these; for I have not proved them.' And David put them off him" (1 Samuel 17:39). In other words David was saying, "I have fought before using my own armor. I have my proven ways to use when I go to battle." It is paramount to use proven formulas rather than strategies that have not been tested. King Saul had not registered any major victories in the past yet he wanted to give David his battle strategies. We should be cautious of the advice we receive and from whom it is being given.

On the other hand, Jesus gave sound advice to His disciples as they faced their own personal battles. His advice was simply, "Wait." It was advice to His fellow laborers in the kingdom of God, a motivation supported by His desire to see them succeed and not fail. One may call the command an executive order given to them before assuming office as successors of His apostolic ministry on the earth.

Waiting is still the most essential key for success given to all apostles of this age. Many fail because they ignore this essential key. Patience is a virtue. The Scriptures declare, "They that wait upon the Lord shall be renewed in strength" (Isaiah 40:31). Impatience may lead to unnecessary difficulty. The story of Joseph provides a classic example of what may happen when one is impatient. Joseph communicated his dream to his brothers before it was time. It is argued Joseph's brothers were jealous, (Genesis 37:5, 8) and though this may be true, Joseph could have waited a bit longer or sought advice from his father on how to more effectively communicate his dream. This could have minimized his suffering at the hands of his brothers. Could it be possible that the way he communicated his dream annoyed his brothers to the extent they decided to eliminate him? Some troubles in life are self-inflicted. Wisdom must be applied at every level to avert unnecessary sufferings (Proverb 4:7).

From a tender age of twelve, Jesus was an eloquent and prolific theologian who confounded teachers with His understanding and exposition of Scriptures. "And all that heard him were astonished at his understanding and answers" (Luke 2:47). Even so, He did not start a ministry at the age of thirteen, He waited for His appointed time.

At an early age Jesus wrought miracles like turning water into wine at a wedding He attended with His mother. He performed a miracle under pressure when His mother asked Him to change water into wine. Judging from His response, He knew it was not yet time to start His ministry. Jesus said to his mother, "Woman, what have I to do with thee? Mine hour is not yet come" (John 2:47). In other words Jesus was in effect saying, "I am a minister in waiting, please don't push Me to get ahead of God's perfect timing." He was patient, never in a hurry. As He began His ministry, Jesus' position was characterized by immense contradictions from His own people; especially the priests, Pharisees, and Sadducees. As a result, He had to be steady, self-composed and have intellectual fortitude.

Our generation believes in an instant philosophy in which everything must happen now. We have products in the market which are doing very well due to their emphasis on instant results: instant coffee, instant noodles, microwave lunches, instant millionaires, and get rich quick pyramid schemes. Such advertising could put pressure on individuals to think they are trailing behind if they do not participate in these instant self gratifications.

In Jesus' apostolic team Judas occupied a key position. But due to his lack of patience and insight, he failed to commit himself to see it through to the end; unaware of the rewards, and the blessings that were to follow those who remained steadfast, obedient, and faithful.

Judas lost out because he could not see beyond where he was. Impatience limits you to now, and robs you of tomorrow. In the passage of scripture below, Jesus clearly outlines the rewards and blessings that follow those who sacrificially given themselves to the work of the kingdom of God.

*And Jesus answered and said, "Verily I say unto you, There is no man that hath left house, or brethren, or sisters, or father, or mother, or wife, or children, or lands, for my sake, and the gospel's, But he shall receive an hundred-fold now in this time, houses, and brethren, and sisters, and mothers, and children, and lands, with persecutions; and in the world to come eternal life." (Mark 10:29-30)*

Betraying the Son of God was the shortest way Judas could see to get his instant benefits. Short cuts are always dangerous and in extreme cases may be the cause of premature death. Impatience cost Judas his position, privileges, blessings, and his due rewards. If his attitude had been right, Judas could have been part of a success story. He could have been listed as one of the founders of the church of Jesus Christ, and part of the apostolic movement that shook the world with signs and wonders. Instead he is remembered only as the one who betrayed the Son of God for thirty pieces of silver.

Patience is the key to blessings and rewards in this world and in the world to come. Let us guard ourselves against the wiles of this world that present what seems good yet is contrary to God's kingdom policy. "For all that is in the world, the lust of the flesh, and the lust of the eyes, and the pride of life, is not of the Father, but is of the world" (1 John 2:16).

The things of this world are temporal and cannot be compared to eternal rewards. "For our light affliction, which is but for a moment, worketh for us a far more exceeding and eternal weight of glory" (2 Corinthians 4:17).

## Jesus Begins His Ministry

The ministry of our Lord Jesus Christ was never to impress people or justify His position in God. He was the Son of God and relied on His father for pronouncement. It's not for a minister to pronounce himself to the world as an ambassador of God, but to wait for his unveiling in the fullness of time.

God has His ways of doing things. He went to the extent of raising up John's ministry to prepare the way and announce the coming of Jesus Christ. The announcement of emerging ministers may sometimes be part of the angels` ministry as it was at the birth of Jesus Christ.

*And the angel said unto them, Fear not: for, behold, I bring you good tidings of great joy, which shall be to all people, for unto you is born this day in the city of David a Savior, which is Christ the Lord. (Luke 2:10-11)*

In raising a ministry, God puts structures in place to counter any obstacles that may arise against its establishment. King David expressed it well when he said, "Thou preparest a table before me in the presence of mine enemies: thou anointest my head with oil; my cup runneth over" (Psalm 23:5). This scripture shows the confidence David had in his God, even in the presence of his enemies.

Indeed God will feed you and cause you to rejoice over your enemies. The anointing of His presence will be upon your life; therefore if God has called you, "wait" for His perfect timing. The passage of scripture below is a good example of what God is willing to do for you when your time has come. Jesse assembled his sons before the Prophet Samuel and knowingly excluded David. Nevertheless, it was David's time so not being in the picture could not stop God from accomplishing His will.

*Again, Jesse made seven of his sons to pass before Samuel. And Samuel said unto Jesse, The LORD hath not chosen these. And Samuel said unto Jesse, Are here all thy children? And he said, There remaineth yet the youngest, and, behold, he keepeth the sheep. And Samuel said unto Jesse, Send and fetch him: for we will not sit down till he come hither. (1 Samuel 16:10-11)*

## God's Announcement

*And suddenly a voice came from heaven, saying, "This is my beloved Son, in whom I am well pleased." (Matthew 3:17 NKJV)*

Why was God so pleased with Jesus? Jesus knew who He was, and who had called Him; He was patient enough to wait for God's time of announcement. In the kingdom of God, the Father himself determines what must take place where, when, and why.

*But when the fullness of time was come, God sent forth his Son, made of a woman, made under the law, To redeem them that were under the law, that we might receive the adoption of sons. (Galatians 4:4-5)*

The other reason God was pleased with Jesus was because of who He was. If biological fathers take pleasure in their own children, how much more will God? God is pleased with all His children, more so when they understand who they are in Him.

*While he yet spake, behold, a bright cloud overshadowed them: and behold a voice out of the cloud, which said, This is my beloved Son, in whom I am well pleased; hear ye him. (Matthew 17:5)*

God was so pleased with Jesus that He qualified His Son to speak for Him, and advised the disciples to listen carefully to Him. Jesus was the express image of God, and if the disciples could hear Him, they could hear God speak. Jesus only spoke of the kingdom of God, and His teachings were with authority. What He saw His father do, that He did also.

As ministers of the gospel, can God say He is pleased with you, can He advise people to listen to you? What teachings can you offer to this generation that you know God has sent you to share? Our generation is in a hurry and requires ministers that are fully equipped in the Word and that have something to say to establish and give godly direction to this generation.

There are some self-appointed apostles who claim to be *favorites* of God, but instead they are actually leading the sheep astray. The Book of Jude has this to say about them: "These are spots in your feasts of charity, when they feast with you, feeding themselves without fear: clouds they are without water, carried about of winds; trees whose fruit withereth, without fruit, twice dead, plucked up by the roots" (Jude 1:12).

The Word of God also calls them deceitful bows in Hosea 7:16, "They return, but not to the most High they are like a deceitful bow their prince shall fall by the sword for the rage of their tongue: this shall be their derision in the land of Egypt." Their day of judgment is coming and they will be no more.

## The Faithfulness of God

*Faithful is he that calleth you, who also will do it. (1 Thessalonians 5:24)*

God is faithful regarding His promises. As a minister you need to know that God does not give and take. In His time He will perform His word concerning you. You can rest in His faithfulness. Wait faithfully for God, for He has promised and given you the assurance that He will never leave you nor forsake you (Hebrews 13:5, Deuteronomy 31:6).

Before commencing His ministry Jesus waited for the baptism of the Holy Spirit. According to the Word, the Holy Spirit came upon Him in the form of a dove and a voice of confirmation spoke so loud that everyone around could hear it. "And Jesus, when he was baptized, went up straightway out of the water: and, lo, the heavens were opened unto him, and he saw the Spirit of God descending like a dove, and lighting upon him: And lo a voice from heaven saying, This is my beloved Son, in whom I am well pleased" (Matthew 3:16-17).

Upon receiving the Holy Spirit, Jesus was led into the wilderness where He was tempted of the devil and He defeated him. The Holy Spirit equips men and women with the power of God, and gives them the ability to do the work of God.

The Holy Spirit comes from God and gives individuals the ability to be witnesses for Him. A witness has first-hand information of an occurrence or event. For a witness to be deemed credible in a court of law, it must be proven beyond reasonable doubt that they actually witnessed the event that occurred. Jesus instructed His disciples to wait for the promised Holy Spirit. Having been baptized in the same manner, Jesus knew the power a minster has from being full of the Holy Spirit. Therefore he said, "Wait for it."

Jesus knew that for His ministry to succeed He had to totally depend on God; He needed to hear from God and put the will of His father above His own. "I can of mine own self do nothing: as I hear, I judge: and my judgment is just; because I seek not mine own will, but the will of the Father which hath sent me" (John 5:30).

To emphasize this let's look at what the Apostle Paul said in 1 Corinthians 2:4, "And my speech and my preaching was not with enticing words of man's wisdom, but in demonstration of the Spirit and of power." The Apostle Paul knew if he was in the center of God's will, grace was going to be available. God can only give you grace when you do what He has called you to do. Spend time with God, allow Him to reveal His purpose for your life, and you will find that grace is available to accomplish His will.

*And how shall they preach, except they be sent? As it is written, how beautiful are the feet of them that preach the gospel of peace, and bring glad tidings of good things! (Romans 10:15)*

The church is the Body of Christ and needs to stay connected to the source of its power to be effective. In the Book of Isaiah the prophet declares, "But they that wait upon the LORD shall renew their strength; they shall mount up with wings as eagles; they shall run, and not be weary; and they shall walk, and not faint" (Isaiah 40:31). The eagle in this passage of scripture is a symbol of strength and power. It is also known as the king among the fowls of the air. The eagle is a royal symbol, therefore those who stay connected to God will live as royalty, reigning in power and authority.

The scripture also speaks about mounting up like an eagle. Mounting in this case denotes an elevation that comes from waiting. Waiting upon God elevates us. Just as the air currents lift the eagle without effort, there is an elevation to places of prominence for those who are willing to wait upon the Lord. Are you struggling to get to the top? Be like an eagle by waiting for and heeding the leadership of the Holy Spirit that dwells within you.

*I will instruct thee and teach thee in the way which thou shalt go: I will guide thee with mine eye. (Psalm 32:8)*

Apostolic people must wait to be sent they don't just wake up and go at will. They know when and how to navigate their ship according to instructions given by the Holy Spirit. The spirit of discernment is their right hand companion. To understand discernment let's take an example from the life of the Apostle Paul. As Paul and other prisoners were sailing to Rome, Paul spoke to the Captain of the ship about their journey. He had perceived the voyage to be with much hurt and damage. However, they all ignored him which resulted in a ship wreck. Some apostles may not be appealing to you, but to ignore an apostolic instruction is tantamount to suicide. The captain of the ship Paul was on lost the ship and the cargo. Lack of apostolic input can result in great loss.

*Teaching them to observe all things whatsoever I have commanded you: and, lo, I am with you always, even unto the end of the world. Amen. (Matthew 28:20)*

Waiting is an apostolic pillar, an anchor to keep us from sailing off course. It cannot be ignored as it is a fundamental truth, an asset, and a companion on the highway of life. To avoid ministerial depression don't run alone. Don't be caught up in a rat race like others who became weary because they ran without divine inspiration and did not make it to their destinies. It is your choice! You can choose to be an eagle, by taking your time, and choosing to fly in the right season.

# Chapter Three

# Unity Is a Key

The kingdom of God operates from a position of cooperation and team work. It is organized so that there is no room for disagreement. One of the best places this is recorded in the Bible is found in the account of creation. Here is how God went about creating the world.

> *And God said, **Let us** make man in our image, after our likeness: and let them have dominion over the fish of the sea, and over the fowl of the air, and over the cattle, and over all the earth, and over every creeping thing that creepeth upon the earth. (Genesis 1:26)*

It is interesting to note how team work brought about everything that we see in the world today. It was the heavenly team that agreed on the creation of the human race. It took team approval for it to be established. You will hear the mention of the Holy Ghost in Genesis 1:2, "And the Spirit of God moved upon the face of the waters." Then God spoke the world into existence. It is indeed the working together of the Godhead that brought about everything that we see in our known world.

There is sufficient evidence to indicate that this was a team effort as we read in Genesis 1:26. "Let **us** make man" indicates plurality not singularity. A multiplicity of ministry versus individual decision making is indicated as the Godhead came to a common decision of establishing what was to be created. At the end of His earthly ministry, our Lord Jesus prayed for His disciples. His main emphasis was that God would make them one as "we are one" referring to the Godhead; God the Father, God the Son, and God the Holy Ghost. He specified that He, His Father and the Holy Ghost were one.

*That they all may be one; as thou, Father, art in me, and I in thee, that they also may be one in us: that the world may believe that thou hast sent me. (John 17:21)*

Jesus worked with a team from the onset. He did not employ a "one-man band" kind of leadership. Instead He involved others developing a winning team. He was familiar with the success of team work hence He did not employ a different strategy or try to re-invent the wheel as He established His church. He copied from the Heavenly pattern set in place from the beginning of creation. Twelve is a governmental number, there are twelve apostles, twelve gates, and there are twelve tribes of Israel. Jesus employed the same method on earth by appointing a twelve-man team.

## Together in One Accord

The church is a body of believers comprised of different members with a diversity of gifts. It functions very well when individuals specialize in their gifting and grace in unity with one another. Church history teaches us that the first New Testament church planted at Jerusalem took off with a big bang. It all started on the day of Pentecost with the infilling of the Holy Spirit as the disciples were gathered together "all with one accord in one place. And suddenly there came a sound from heaven as of a rushing mighty wind, and it filled all the house where they were sitting" (Acts 2:1-2).

There was a great influx of people added to the church after that; the growth was significant. One of the key things that attracted people to want to be part of the New Testament church was their sweet spirit of togetherness and unity. It was so evident and tangible that no one dared to ignore it. The technology of their media had not reached the levels of media in our modern world, but that alone was not a negative influence in regards to the growth of the church. Even though they had no television or any other electronic media, they made a significant impact in the world. The reason for this success is recorded in Act 2:37- 41.

*Now when they heard this, they were pricked in their heart, and said unto Peter and to the rest of the apostles, Men and brethren, what shall we do? Then Peter said unto them, Repent, and be baptized every one of you in the name of Jesus Christ for the remission of sins, and ye shall receive the gift of the Holy Ghost. For the promise is unto you, and to your children, and to all that are afar off, even as many as the Lord our God shall call, And with many other words did he testify and exhort, saying, Save yourselves from this untoward generation. Then they that gladly received his word were baptized: and the same day there were added unto them about three thousand souls.*

Their influence was broad. It impacted various communities including the business world. This was the prototype church that permanently transformed the whole world. The secret that brought the transformation was embodied in the prayer of our Lord Jesus, when He prayed in John 17:21, "That they all may be one; as thou, Father, art in me, and I in thee, that they also may be one in us: that the world may believe that thou hast sent me."

This is how the events unfolded. It was through a group of people that came together and united in vision, in faith, and in purpose. This all took place just after the assassination and ascension of Jesus. In their fear they hid in an upper room and united in prayer. They prayed in one accord. There is something special that happens when people unite in prayer and call upon the name of the Lord. It is one of the pictures the Bible paints for us that pleases our Heavenly Father. It is a true reflection of what takes place around the throne of God. Heaven is a place of unity; those who are not in unity are demoted and sent out from the presence of God. Lucifer found himself out of the united kingdom of the Father, Son, and Holy Ghost due to his attempts to bring disunity.

There is nothing that moves the heart of God as much as seeing His people in unity. Unity is a true picture of heaven. When Lucifer wanted to introduce a new doctrine of disunity, immediately God fired him, and expelled him from heaven. Heaven has no place for disunity.

## Unity is Power

We see another picture of the power of unity at the tower of Babel when people decided to build a tower to reach Heaven (Genesis 11:1-9). It is not known or recorded what levels of engineering and architectural capability those early people possessed. However, from the scriptural point of view it is said that God had to intervene in order to stop the construction of a tower that was destined to reach as high as Heaven. Based on that information we are given, one would say it looked possible that this construction would have become a reality. If not, there would have been no need for God to come down and stop them. These people are said to be those that had one mind and one language. Whatever they wanted to do was within their reach. In short they were united.

Indeed there is nothing people who are united cannot accomplish. There is a saying, "unity is power." Unity is also strength. Without it God's people and the world at large would not survive at all. The Babel project was going to be a success because of the unity that existed among those people. It took the same united team of the Father and the host of heaven to come and stop them. That's what our brethren in West African countries would refer to as "fire for fire." The forces of heaven had to come and stop this group of people on the earth who wanted to build a master piece. Even though their motive was wrong, their strategy was right. To counter what the people had planned, God and the heavenly host had to employ a similar strategy and in the same spirit heaven and earth were created.

We see complete harmony and agreement in that unity which is confirmed when God said, "Let Us create." As the triune God continued with creation, each time a phase was completed God said that which came out of that unity was good. Unity is the source of all goodness. The absence of goodness in our lives requires that we check how much we are in unity with everything around us. We must be in unity with our fellow man, as well as with our heavenly Father; that will enable us to accomplish our God-given assignment.

How much are you in agreement with God, your apostolic family, and those around you? Could it be possible that some of the defeats that you are suffering in your life are a direct result of not working in unity with your church family? Don't be a partaker in strife that will harm the efforts of what the church is trying to achieve. Anyone who causes strife within the Body of Christ will find they are excluded from the spiritual family as well as the heavenly family. Indeed God will not endorse what is done outside of unity. Take heed that you don't bring upon yourself a swift judgment by not working in agreement with the church community and with heaven's agenda.

Disunity is the root of all defeat. The lack of goodness in us may be due to the fact that we are disconnected from God. The scripture declares, "behold the hand of the Lord is not shortened that it cannot save but our sins have separated us from God" (Isaiah 59:1). Do not be in disunity even with your God given conscience. God warned Cain in Genesis 4:7, "If you do well, you will be happy and if you do not evil is at the door" (author paraphrase).

The goodness of God does not come until we are one with God our creator. The goodness of the Lord makes one rich and adds no sorrow. There is no uglier picture than a disunited people, home, church, or country.

## Disunity is a Nightmare

Satan is the father of disunity. He uses the strategy of divide and conquer and has since before his dismissal from heaven. He planted one agent in the apostolic team of our Lord Jesus to try to create disunity among them and the results were catastrophic. His name was Judas Iscariot

*For all that is in the world, the lust of the flesh, and the lust of the eyes, and the pride of life, is not of the Father, but is of the world. (1 John 2:16).*

Be prayerful and guard yourselves so you will not be used by Satan to sow seeds of disunity. Some of the things Satan will use to bring disunity are greed, love of money, and lust. Judas was motivated by love of money. When he "sold" Jesus, the Son of the living God for thirty pieces of silver, his life ended in tragedy.

*Now this man purchased a field with the reward of iniquity; and falling headlong, he burst asunder in the midst, and all his bowels gushed out. (Acts 1:18)*

Judas, though he was one of the disciples of Jesus, was motivated by selfishness and ended up betraying the Son of God. Operating in the spirit of disunity, he betrayed not only the Son of God but the whole apostolic team. The team was scattered and as a result of this disunity, a blessed apostolic team that had been moving in the power of God was brought to a standstill. Disunity can stop the power of God from moving among His people. In the midst of disunity people backslide.

*Now Peter sat without in the palace: and a damsel came unto him, saying, Thou also wast with Jesus of Galilee. But he denied before them all, saying, I know not what thou sayest.* (Matthew 26:69-70)

The spirit of disunity often targets those that are in leadership so that when the shepherd is struck down the sheep scatter. Peter denied Jesus under pressure. Fear, hiding, and relocation are the immediate results of the spirit of disunity. We see this in the lives of the disciples of Jesus soon after He was crucified. A devastating scattering occurred as they headed off in different directions. Some went to the nearby cities and towns while others went to the upper room to pray.

Upon rising from the dead, the first thing Jesus did was to reassemble and reunite His disciples so they would be prepared to go and preach the gospel. Those that are in the ministry of preaching the gospel must seek after unity. Unity can bring the nations back to God.

Jesus began to manifest Himself mightily through the ministry of His united apostles. When he had successfully brought them together Jesus showed up in their ministry in an unprecedented way. People from all walks of life began to join them. Some sold their farms and their businesses to become part of the great united apostolic movement.

When this small group of people who were hiding in an upper room responded to the call of unity and began to pray, the church grew bigger by the day and consequently became a united people. On the day of their debut into ministry, three thousand came to join them. Their launch was not a fancy one. It was so unprofessional that those who witnessed it at first said thought they were drunk. Even though the disciples looked like they were drunk, when the people heard the power of their testimony, many wanted to sign up and join them. The power of their unity was so real and genuine; people couldn't wait to be part of this great church. Could it be that sometimes people don't want to come and join us because we are not united? True unity is contagious!

## Unity is Like the Anointing Oil

> *Behold, how good and how pleasant it is for brethren to dwell together in unity! It is like the precious ointment upon the head, that ran down upon the beard, even Aaron's beard: that went down to the skirts of his garments; As the dew of Hermon, and as the dew that descended upon the mountains of Zion: for there the LORD commanded the blessing, even life for evermore. (Psalm 133:1-3)*

In Psalm 133, the psalmist speaks a great deal on the matter of unity. He says unity is like anointing oil, it is good and it is pleasant. He goes on to say when brethren dwell together in unity it pleases God. He refers to unity as precious oil like that which was used on Aaron's head. The oil that was used by Moses to anoint Aaron's head was a mixture of five key ingredients that God ordered Moses to use. These ingredients were united together, symbolic of unity, and the psalmist calls that a "precious oil." When unity is in place people cease to be common;

they become precious and powerful. A house divided cannot stand.

There were five ingredients that Moses used to make this precious anointing oil. Five is often referred to as an apostolic number. There are five ministry gifts in the church of our Lord Jesus. The oil represents the anointing that will be prevalent in the church when the church operates in unity and it will not run short of gifts. The ingredients that made up the oil were precious; every gift that God brings into the church is precious. The precious oil is that which God will use to build His united body as the church.

In Genesis 1:27-28, God spoke the five fold mission and the blessings to the first man He had just created: fruitfulness, multiplication, subduing, replenishing and dominion. A true apostolic church is not a barren church, it is known by its productivity. Lack of productivity is a sign that unity is lacking. Fruitfulness is a sign that we are walking in the blessings of God.

> *Beware of false prophets, which come to you in sheep's clothing, but inwardly they are ravening wolves. Ye shall know them by their fruits. Do men gather grapes of thorns, or figs of thistles? (Matthew 7:15-16)*

The Bible declares that we shall be known by our fruit. The apostolic people of God, the sent ones, are known by the good fruit they produce. There are a lot of messed up people that have gone out in the name of the Lord. The Bible says we must test all the spirits because not all spirits are from God. One of the ways we can test these spirits is by looking at the fruit they produce. "Therefore by their fruits you will know them" (Matthew 7:20 NKJV).

## Fruitfulness

*"I am the Vine; you are the branches. Whoever lives in Me and I in him bears much (abundant) fruit. However, apart from Me [cut off from vital union with Me] you can do nothing." (John 15:5 AMP)*

In the Book of John, Jesus speaks of being the Vine and us as the branches. He went on to say every branch that does not produce will be cut off. One of the reasons people are not fruitful is lack of alignment and connectivity with the entire body. Every joint, eye, hand and foot must supply according to its ability in order for the body to properly function.

*For as in one physical body we have many parts (organs, members) and all of these parts do not have the same function or use, so we, numerous as we are, are one body in Christ (the Messiah) and individually we are parts one of another [mutually dependent on one another]. Having gifts (faculties, talents, qualities) that differ according to the grace given us, let us use them..." (Romans 12:4-6 AMP)*

God has placed us in the Body and has granted us different grace, abilities, and talents. He desires us to use these gifts to be fruitful. That simply means being what He created us to be. There are a number of Scriptures that speak of being fruitful. Fruit speaks of your ability, your character, your integrity, and who you are in God. In Jesus said, "You shall know them by their fruit" (Matthew 7:20). The world is full of church goers who have nothing to show for their faith. However, the true citizens of heaven are known by their Christ-like lifestyle. They are not known for their Sunday morning or special holiday gatherings. They are known for being like Christ in the market place. No matter where they are they bear the true marks of what Christ would be if He was on the earth today. Through their words and actions they can be easily identified. Their fruit speaks of the life of Christ in them.

> *But the fruit of the Spirit is love, joy, peace, longsuffering, gentleness, goodness, faith, meekness, temperance: against such there is no law. (Galatians 5:22-23)*

True Christianity has fruit. You cannot claim to be a child of God without love and all the other attributes mentioned in the scripture above. These attributes are the evidence that one is walking in the unity of the Spirit of God.

## Multiplication

God's creation is to be fruitful and multiply. This

simply shows us that God's intention has always been to see progression in multiples. In other words He wants to see maximum results from everything He created. He desires to see that each living thing begins to reproduce after its own kind, in multiples. The decree of blessing of fruitfulness and multiplication was bestowed upon the first man God created in Genesis. In a similar statement in the New Testament, our Lord Jesus said, "I chose you and appointed you to go and bear fruit—fruit that will last..." (John 15:16 NIV). The word "go" is an apostolic term that is also found in the great commission as the Lord was sending His apostolic people to the nations in Mark 16:15. If the church, the Body of Christ is told to "go into all the world" then we should be able to see its universal multiplication. The intention of God is not to see denominational or religious multiplication. He desires to see the Body of Christ increase until the whole world becomes encompassed in the kingdom of God; every nation on every continent. When God says *all* He means *all*!

I don't share the view that I once saw in the Cape region in South Africa where certain churches have restricted themselves to meeting in the basement or in the backyards of their membership. They gather playing backtracks of popular gospel bands and claim that they cannot fit into the local churches. To me that's disunity and should not be what the church stands for. There is nothing wrong with family members meeting together, but that should not be done to the extent that it brings disunity the Body of Christ.

I have seen people who do not agree with the

vision of their local church so they feel they should start their own church, and channel their money where they feel it's best used for the Lord's work. I also don't share the view that the size of your contribution qualifies one to hold a church office or that one should start their own church. Financial contribution doesn't buy you a church post or a gift in the fivefold ministry. This is descriptive of disunity and steals the blessings of the gospel of Christ which unites and not divides. The church is not a burial society or a "bless me" club.

## Subdue

> *And God blessed them and said to them, Be fruitful, multiply, and fill the earth, and* **subdue it [using all its vast resources in the service of God and man];** *and have dominion over the fish of the sea, the birds of the air, and over every living creature that moves upon the earth. (Genesis 1:28 AMP emphasis added)*

The church is also commanded to subdue the world which means to have influence beyond our region. The dictionary definition of subdue is, "to conquer, overcome, and bring under control or the extension of superior power." Therefore the church must be influential even to the degree that it affects the other parts of the world as well as our families, schools, universities, and businesses. We must influence those that are near and far. Our Commander in Chief said we shall be His witnesses from Jerusalem to the uttermost parts of the world. He also said He was sending the Holy Spirit to us so we would have the power and authority to do just that.

> *But you shall receive power (ability, efficiency, and might) when the Holy Spirit has come upon you, and you shall be My witnesses in Jerusalem and all Judea and Samaria and to the ends (the very bounds) of the earth. (Acts 1:8 AMP)*

Jesus also assured His disciples that He had been given the power to not only subdue the earth; He also had the authority to pass that power on to them, and send them out to continue the work that He started.

> *Jesus approached and, breaking the silence, said to them, **All authority** (all power of rule) in heaven and on earth has been given to Me. Go then and make disciples of all the nations, baptizing them into the name of the Father and of the Son and of the Holy Spirit, Teaching them to observe everything that I have commanded you, and behold, I am with you all the days (perpetually, uniformly, and on every occasion), to the [very] close and consummation of the age. Amen (so let it be). (Matthew 28:18-20 AMP emphasis added)*

## Replenish

> *And God blessed them, and God said unto them, Be fruitful, and multiply, and **replenish***

> ***the earth***, *and subdue it: and have dominion over the fish of the sea, and over the fowl of the air, and over every living thing that moveth upon the earth. (Genesis 1:28 emphasis added)*

The word "replenish" means to fill something up again, to supply fully, to fill with inspiration or power, to build-up again, to make good, or to replace. When God created the human being He gave him the ability to reproduce so that through mankind what God has begun would continue to be revealed. After God creates something He closes the factory and leaves the power of reproduction to that which He has created. Therefore, there is re-creation power that flows through unity. Hence the word replenish is synonymous with the workings of God as explained in this chapter.

When God created the first man, it is clear that he was on the supplier's side; not on the consumer's side. He lacked nothing. The purpose of his existence was to compliment and define what God had created. He came to the earth to replenish it. He had no need, he lacked nothing. He lived in the middle of plenty until he lost it all due to sin. Therefore, the restoration of the fallen man should bring him back into that position whereby he functions in the capacity of refilling that which was emptied due to the Adamic fall.

Man can only replenish the earth when his relationship with God is re-established. Man was not created to beg, live in lack, isolation, distress, and wander the earth in lack of divine direction. Adam found himself naked and began to look for fig leaves to cover his shame. Then he went and hid from the presence of God. He had fallen from the position of supply and had become bankrupt because of sin. However, God's intention was always for mankind to be on the replenishing side using the divine capabilities that were deposited in him upon creation.

*According as **his divine power hath given unto us all things that pertain unto life and godliness,** through the knowledge of him that hath called us to glory and virtue: Whereby are given unto us exceeding great and precious promises: that by these ye might be partakers of the divine nature, having escaped the corruption that is in the world through lust. (2 Peter 1:3-4 emphasis added)*

What Adam lost when he fell into sin, Jesus regained through His obedience even unto the cross. He has the authority to send out His Body to not only replenish it but also have dominion over the earth and fulfill the original commandment given to us on the day of creation.

## Dominion

*For I reckon that the sufferings of this present time are not worthy to be compared with the glory which shall be revealed in us. For the earnest expectation of the creature waiteth for the manifestation of the sons of God. For the creature was made subject to vanity, not willingly, but by reason of him who hath subjected the same in hope, (Romans 8:18-20)*

God created us to have dominion, to be rulers, and to be in charge. He gave us a place on the earth to exercise our ruler-ship. That place is none other than the church.

*And hath made us kings and priests unto God and his Father; to him be glory and dominion for ever and ever. Amen. (Revelation 1:6)*

Man is a king under the King of kings. We are co-workers with Christ. The Bible declares that the saints shall take the kingdom and shall reign forever. Every child of God must be praying and preparing for a takeover. It must be clear that as a child of God we already have dominion in heavenly places, even the host of the dark kingdom is aware that it is subject to us in the spiritual realm.

The New Testament apostolic movement became a voice on the earth. It became difficult for the government of that time to stop them from influencing the people with the gospel of Jesus Christ. They were accused of turning the world upside down (Acts 17:6). Their influence was so strong that many communities came to them for answers. The present day apostolic movement carries a governmental anointing and it is to rule on the earth. Today's church should also be consistently accused of "turning the world upside down."

The church is the hope of the world because Christ in us is the hope of glory. The beauty and the splendor of our God must be seen through us. That will happen when the kingdom of God has been practically revealed in and through us. The scripture declares that the kingdom of God must come on earth as it is in heaven.

> *After this manner therefore pray ye: Our Father which art in heaven, Hallowed be thy name. Thy kingdom come. Thy will be done in earth, as it is in heaven. (Matthew 6:9-10)*

### The Universal Power of Unity

The church is the catholic church of God, and it is the universal united church of our Lord Jesus Christ. I am not talking about the Roman Catholic religion. I am talking about the whole body of Christ on the earth. This only happens when we understand the power of unity. Even our religious titles do not matter in this regard. The whole world can experience a global revival and a great harvest of souls through such unity.

> *If my people, which are called by my name, shall humble themselves, and pray, and seek my face, and turn from their wicked ways;*

> *then will I hear from heaven, and will for-*
> *give their sin, and will heal their land.*
> *(2 Chronicles 7:14)*

If the people of God unite, and pray, and seek God's face; God has promised He will hear from heaven and will heal our land. The whole of creation is groaning and is waiting for the manifestation of the united apostolic church.

Unity is the kingdom's master key. The whole mission of our Lord Jesus on earth was to reconcile man to God. God was in Christ reconciling and uniting the whole world with Him. It took the Son of God to die on the cross for the reunification of mankind to God. God was bringing His family that was living in disunity back to Him.

There was a disintegration of relationship between men and God. "That at that time ye were without Christ, being aliens from the commonwealth of Israel, and strangers from the covenants of promise, having no hope, and without God in the world: But now in Christ Jesus ye who sometimes were far off are made nigh by the blood of Christ" (Ephesians 2:12-13). That speaks of reconciliation and unity. We are one body though we are many. We are one body in Christ.

> *For he is our peace, who hath made both one,*
> *and hath broken down the middle wall of par-*
> *tition between us. (Ephesians 2:14)*

Christ's death on the cross was very symbolic. His lifted hands spoke of reaching out to the dying world, and reaching out to God saying, "Be reconciled."

> *Having abolished in his flesh the enmity, even the law of commandments contained in ordinances; for to make in himself of twain one new man, so making peace; And **that he might reconcile both unto God in one body by the cross**, having slain the enmity thereby. (Ephesians 2:15-16 emphasis added)*

Unity is an anointing, it is good, it is pleasant, and it has a fivefold ministry emphasis.

# Chapter Four

# Prophecy the Apostolic Master Keys

I am a product of the prophetic ministry. I strongly believe that God is still speaking today through this ministry. I have received countless prophecies from the time I gave my life to the Lord. One of the prophecies came just weeks after my conversion. I recall I was spending time in prayer in the woods when I got a direct and clear prophecy that I was to go and ask my pastor for an opportunity to preach in our church. This message came to me in tongues, and I understood very clearly what I was to preach. That evening I went to my pastor, I told him about my encounter with God and what He had instructed me to say. When I had finished telling him my story, the pastor told me he would give me time to minister at our midweek service on Wednesday. Little did I know that this was to be the beginning of many such opportunities to follow in my walk of faith. Wednesday night came and it was my first time ever to stand before people and preach. I thank

God for my pastor who had faith in me.

In my Islamic background, such things never happened. Here I was standing before my elders, preaching to a people I knew had much experience and were more mature in the things of God than I was. Indeed there is power in the prophetic and God is always ready to perform His Word. I only took about forty-five minutes and have no idea what came over me. Surely the spirit of prophecy was at work, word for word. What God had told me when I prayed alone in the bush came to my memory as I delivered my sermon. I now know it is known as prophetic preaching. It was the best night of my life and one that I will never forget as long as I live. When I finished preaching I gave an altar call, and many that were in the service came to the front for prayer, both young and old.

My peers were so proud of me. They all wanted to know how I had done it. The highlight of that night was one gentleman who came to the front for prayer. He gave testimony of how the message preached had brought about conviction in his heart because for a long time he had been running away from his calling. In the days following my message, this man said he was going to resign from his work and would become a full time minister saying, "I am going to take the Word of the Lord seriously from this moment on."

It was indeed prophetic preaching that brought him to that decision. It was not me speaking; I was just a mouth piece for God. God was giving His instruction through me.

*The lion hath roared, who will not fear? The Lord GOD hath spoken, who can but prophesy? (Amos 3:8)*

Prophecy is for today, it is needed even more in the modern church of our Lord Jesus Christ. The prophetic ministry is one of the gifts released to the New Testament Church. When there was the outpouring of the Holy Spirit at Pentecost, prophecy was released. All believers are required to partake of it. The outpouring of the Holy Spirit was prophesied of by Joel in the Old Testament.

*And it shall come to pass afterward, that I will pour out my spirit upon all flesh; and your sons and your daughters shall prophesy, your old men shall dream dreams, your young men shall see visions: And also upon the servants and upon the handmaids in those days will I pour out my spirit. (Joel 2:28-29)*

However, there is a need to redefine the New Testament prophetic ministry versus that of the Old Testament, as there is a slight difference in their operation and functions. There has been a lot of misunderstanding regarding the subject of prophecy among believers across the board. Let us take a look at how the Old and New Testament Prophets functioned.

First and foremost, every prophetic gift operates under the unction of the Holy Ghost.

*But ye have an unction from the Holy One, and ye know all things. (1 John 2:20) And his father Zacharias was filled with the Holy Ghost, and prophesied, saying, Blessed be the Lord God of Israel; for he hath visited and redeemed his people, and hath raised up an horn of salvation for us in the house of his servant David; as he spake by the mouth of his holy prophets, which have been since the world began. (Luke 1:67-70)*

However, to prophesy under the unction of the Holy Spirit does not necessarily make one a prophet as stated in 1 Corinthians 12:29, "Are all apostles? Are all prophets? Are all teachers? Are all workers of miracles?" A prophet as defined in the Webster's Dictionary is defined as, "predicting the future under the influence of Divine guidance." There are several words in scripture used to refer to prophecy. The Old Testament Hebrew word for prophecy is *Chazah* which means to gaze at, to perceive mentally, contemplate (with pleasure), to have a vision of, to see, behold with an eye, to see a seer in the ecstatic state.

**Listed below are examples of the different ways to explain prophecy.**

Behold - Job 23:9; Psalms 17:2, 27:4
Look – Isaiah 33:20; Micah 4:11
Prophesy – Isaiah 30:10
Provide – Exodus 18:21

(Also see Isaiah 1:1; Ezekiel 13:6-8; Habakkuk 1:1; and Zechariah 10:2.)

Apostles and prophets work hand in hand. The Scriptures state that the church is founded upon the apostolic and prophetic foundation. These are the two key ministries upon which the church is built. They are also the two key ministries that are most misunderstood and most persecuted. They are governmental by nature. Their main function is to give direction and insight to the church. Prophecy and the Holy Spirit function in harmony as mentioned in the paragraphs above. The prophecy by Joel pointed to a time when the Holy Spirit would be poured out upon all flesh. The New Testament's prophetic people are not classified by age or gender, as the prophetic message in Joel clearly points out: "I will pour out my spirit upon all flesh; and your sons and your daughters shall prophesy."

We are living in the most exciting days where everyone who has accepted Jesus Christ as their personal Savior can have access to the Spirit of prophecy dwelling in them. When the prophetic anointing is present it eliminates all modes of discrimination, irrelevant people become relevant, and it raises "nobodies" to "somebodies."

Religion has often had an issue when it comes to age and tribe. In the Book of Samuel when Saul prophesied it raised some concerns among the people.

*And it came to pass, when all that knew him beforetime saw that, behold, he prophesied among the prophets, then the people said one to another, What is this that is come unto the son of Kish? Is Saul also among the prophets? (1 Samuel 10:11)*

Not everyone was expected to function as a prophet under the Old Testament order. Prophets were referred to as servants of Jehovah. They were His mouthpieces through which people would inquire of God. Prophets were raised and chosen by God, it was never left to the individual to just wake up one day and call themselves a prophet. In the New Testament however, both the young and old are qualified by the infilling of the Holy Ghost in their new relationship with Jesus.

*And I fell at his feet to worship him. **And he said unto me, See thou do it not: I am thy fellow servant, and of thy brethren that have the testimony of Jesus:** worship God: for the testimony of Jesus is the spirit of prophecy. (Revelation 19:10 emphasis added)*

### Degrees of Prophetic Inspiration

Prophecy is an inspirational utterance from the Holy Spirit through an individual as the Spirit wills. The Spirit of prophecy was evident in the genealogy from Adam to Moses.

   a.  Adam prophesied concerning his bride and the marriage state (Genesis 2:20-25).

b.  Enoch prophesied of the second coming of Christ (Jude 14, 15).

c.  Noah was a preacher of righteousness because the Spirit of Christ upon him (2 Peter 2:5, Hebrews 11:7, 1 Peter 3:20).

d.  Abraham was spoken of as a prophet (Genesis 20:7).

e.  Isaac and Jacob had the Spirit of prophecy upon them as they blessed their son's (Genesis 27, 48, 49; Hebrews 11:20-21; Psalm 105:9-15)

f.  Joseph prophesied of the exodus from Egypt (Genesis 50:24, Hebrews 11:22)

At times the Spirit of prophecy fell upon groups of people (see Numbers 11:24-30). The Lord took the Spirit that was upon Moses and placed it upon seventy of the elders of Israel and they prophesied. The Spirit of prophecy fell upon Saul and all his messengers. Saul was not among the prophets but he still came under the influence of the Spirit of prophecy (see 1 Samuel 19:20-24 and 10:10). Prophesying was evidence of the presence of God's Spirit on an individual in the Old Testament. In our present day meetings if the Spirit of God wills, the Spirit of prophecy is released.

*And it shall come to pass afterward, that I will pour out my spirit upon all flesh; and your sons and your daughters shall prophesy, your old men shall dream dreams, your young men shall see visions. (Joel 2:28)*

This prophecy demonstrates that when the Holy Spirit comes He brings about a total transformation; a release of a prophetic people living under the unction of the Holy Spirit. According to Joel, it was through the out pouring of the Holy Spirit that the prophetic would be released. No one can prophesy without the Holy Spirit. In the Old Testament, holy men of God spoke as the Spirit of God gave them utterance. When the Spirit of God comes upon people they begin to function prophetically.

*Of which salvation the prophets have enquired and searched diligently, who prophesied of the grace that should come unto you: Searching what, or what manner of time the Spirit of Christ which was in them did signify, when it testified beforehand the sufferings of Christ, and the glory that should follow. (1 Peter 1:11)*

Prophecy should not only be viewed as giving the word of the Lord or predicting the future, rather it must be treated as a life style. Prophecy must be in all areas of our lives. The Spirit of prophecy is also released through music. David operated in the prophetic as a young man playing his harp. He would be called upon to play for Saul whenever an evil spirit was upon him.

*And Saul's servants said unto him, Behold now, an evil spirit from God troubleth thee. Let our lord now command thy servants, which are before thee, to seek out a man, who is a cunning player on an harp: and it shall come to pass, when the evil spirit from God is upon thee, that he shall play with his hand, and thou shalt be well. (1 Samuel 16:15-16)*

## Prophetic Music

When music is played prophetically it can set people free from their bondages. Prophetic music is very powerful, it releases healing and liberty to people who are under Satan's attack.

*And it came to pass, when the evil spirit from God was upon Saul, that David took a harp, and played with his hand: so Saul was refreshed, and was well, and the evil spirit departed from him. (1 Samuel 16:23)*

Prophetic anointing changes people's lives and has the grace to bring about instant transformation.

*And it came to pass, when all that knew him before time saw that, behold, he prophesied among the prophets, then the people said one to another, What is this that is come unto the son of Kish? Is Saul also among the prophets? (1 Samuel 10:11)*

Dancing is also part of the prophetic. When one is dancing, it signifies celebration and excitement.

The devil brings challenges our way to devastate and demoralize us, it is therefore important to respond by prophetically dancing and rejoicing. Even the Scriptures declare that the joy of the Lord is our strength. When we rejoice in the most difficult times, we are prophetically declaring positive results versus allowing the negative circumstances of where we are to overcome us. David, as an Old Testament prophet, danced because he understood the significance of music in the kingdom of God. "And David danced before the LORD with all his might; and David was girded with a linen ephod" (2 Samuel 6:14).

A time is coming, where the prophetic people of God will not respond to what is happening naturally, rather they will openly respond only to what the prophetic is saying. The word of the Lord declares, let the weak say I am strong and let the poor say I am rich (Joel 3:10). In the same spirit of prophetic singing, Moses was also listed among the people that would sing to the Lord.

"Then sang Moses and the children of Israel this song unto the LORD, and spake, saying, I will sing unto the LORD, for he hath triumphed gloriously: the horse and his rider hath he thrown into the sea" (Exodus 15:1).

Allow me to say that music is a companion of the prophets. Even in heaven there will be music, therefore, those that are heaven bound must be acquainted with the fact that heaven is a musical environment. Music was part of the prophetic culture in the Old Testament church and it will continue to be throughout the 21st century New Testament Church.

In Numbers 11:29, Moses spoke these words to the Old Testament believers, "And Moses said unto him, Enviest thou for my sake? Would God that all the LORD'S people were prophets, and that the LORD would put his spirit upon them!" Moses understood the importance of the prophetic anointing. His emphasis was that this anointing should not be limited to a few individuals because of the tremendous blessings and breakthroughs it entails.

At one point, Moses spent a substantial amount of time in the presence of God on the Mountain of Sinai. From that experience he discovered what it meant to hear from God and the benefits of being in His presence. It is recorded in Exodus 34:29 that when he came down from the mountain even his countenance had changed. "And it came to pass, when Moses came down from mount Sinai with the two tables of testimony in Moses' hand, when he came down from the mount, that Moses wist not that the skin of his face shone while he talked with him."

The presence of God is transformational as is seen in the case of Moses where the skin of his face shone. I would like to believe that when he outlined the fact that he wished all God's people to be prophets, he was referring to his personal experience.

## The Transforming Power of the Prophetic

The prophetic has the ability to change lives. Nations can be elevated into places of prominence when the prophetic word of God is spoken over them.

*And they rose early in the morning, and went forth into the wilderness of Tekoa: and as they went forth, Jehoshaphat stood and said, Hear me, O Judah, and ye inhabitants of Jerusalem; Believe in the LORD your God, so shall ye be established; believe his prophets, so shall ye prosper. (2 Chronicles 20:20)*

One of the things the prophetic word will do is establish people and cause them to prosper. God wants His people to prosper. One of the ways He prospers His people is through the prophetic, on the condition that they believe. Prophets must be believed and not persecuted. The Spirit of God must not be restricted but must be received. When that takes place, God begins to dwell among His people. Hence the Bible declares in 1 Thessalonians 5:19, "Quench not the Spirit." And in Psalm 105:15, "Touch not mine anointed, and do my prophets no harm."

The statement of Moses that he wished all God's people to be prophets was an all encompassing statement that spoke of the time he lived in and the people he was addressing. It also spoke about the future of God's people with regard to everyone having access to God. All must have the same access when it comes to the matter of hearing from God. Moses knew prophetically a day was indeed coming that in the economy of God there would be a generation that would hear and depend on the voice of God. God does not want to hide what He is doing from His people as the scripture declares in Amos 3:7, "Surely the Lord GOD will do nothing, but he revealeth his secret unto his servants the prophets."

After spending forty days on the mountain, Moses had firsthand experience of how it felt to be in the presence of God. He had a full taste of the glory of heaven. Once you have tasted the glory and the presence and once you have heard God speak, you want to stay there forever. Moses prayed to God and said, "And he said unto him, If thy presence go not with me, carry us not up hence" (Exodus 33:15). Once you have tasted the glory it is difficult to imagine living without it.

A similar incident occurred when Jesus took Peter and John to the Mount of Transfiguration. Jesus was transfigured right before their eyes. That incident had such impact on them Peter had no idea what to say. "Then answered Peter, and said unto Jesus, Lord, it is good for us to be here: if thou wilt, let us make here three tabernacles; one for thee, and one for Moses, and one for Elias." (Matthew 17:4).

Their perception of Jesus was no longer the same. There is nothing like being in the presence of God. It totally changes you. After seeing the beauty of the transfiguration, Peter wanted to build a tabernacle for the two prophets, Moses and Elias because he wanted that prophetic experience to be permanent. It is a fact that not only was Jesus transfigured, the Apostles were also transfigured. A prophetic realm is guaranteed to change people's lives as Peter recorded in 2 Peter 1:16-19.

*For we have not followed cunningly devised fables, when we made known unto you the power and coming of our Lord Jesus Christ, but were eyewitnesses of his majesty. For he received from God the Father honour and glory, when there came such a voice to him from the excellent glory, This is my beloved Son, in whom I am well pleased. And this voice which came from heaven we heard, when we were with him in the holy mount. We have also a more sure word of prophecy; whereunto ye do well that ye take heed, as unto a light that shineth in a dark place, until the day dawn, and the day star arise in your hearts.*

This is what Peter had to say concerning his eye witness account of his mountain top experience. The prophetic speaks of what God has revealed by His Spirit making His prophetic people become His witnesses. Jesus addressed His disciples before He ascended into heaven saying, "But ye shall receive power, after that the Holy Ghost is come upon you: and ye shall be witnesses unto me both in Jerusalem, and in all Judaea, and in Samaria, and unto the uttermost part of the earth" (Acts 1:8).

The prophetic is a preview of what is to come. It activates your faith levels and positions you in a place of expectation and enables you to believe God for what He is bringing to you. The prophetic has the ability to fill you with hope, courage and faith while providing you godly values to live by.

## Understanding the Prophetic Ministry

Prophecy must be desired and not be perceived as something negative and suspicious. One of the reasons people don't follow after the prophetic is because of how it has been misrepresented and misunderstood. There have been a lot of misconceptions regarding this ministry and much teaching must be done to re-address the misconceptions so that people can see the positive side of the prophetic and the blessings it carries. According to the Apostle Paul prophesy is the most edifying, comforting and encouraging ministry. "Follow after charity, and desire spiritual gifts, but rather that ye may prophesy" (1 Corinthians 14:1).

When Moses was on the verge of giving up and going through personal ministerial depression, God gave him what one may call a prophetic antidote.

*And the LORD came down in a cloud, and spake unto him, and took of the spirit that was upon him, and gave it unto the seventy elders: and it came to pass, that, when the spirit rested upon them, they prophesied, and did not cease. (Numbers 11:25)*

God extended an invitation to the elders of the Israelites to participate in the same prophetic ministry that was upon Moses. The prophetic anointing was the key that was going to allow Moses to have the manpower that would help him carry the burden of ministry. God ordered him to bring all the elders and said, "I will take the spirit that is upon you and I will give it to them." This scripture reveals that there was an immediate transfer and manifestation of the prophetic anointing upon the leaders and they could not stop prophesying.

God wants His people to continually flow in the prophetic. Hearing from God should not be seasonal, it must be an ongoing phenomena. When God ceases to speak to His people and when His people cease to hear from Him, Satan and his host begin to capitalize on that. Counterfeit spirits and false teachings are inevitable. In the absence of the prophetic people stray or are misled.

The prophetic anointing is a burden bearing anointing. Are you burdened? Are the trials of this world wearing you down? God has ordained the prophetic anointing to get rid of all the worries of this world. Moses said it was his wish that all God's people would be prophetic. There is nothing you cannot go through when the prophetic grace is upon you. It gives you the grace to look forward to something new. As long as you have a promise that is pending, the devil will try all he can but he can't have you. Moses knew that the people of God would need the prophetic to help them successfully go through hardships.

On the other hand, there was an incident when Elisha was surrounded by enemies. His assistant panicked and asked Elisha, "What are we going to do?" The prophetic takes away panic and puts you at ease. It opens your spiritual eyes and makes you see beyond your natural limitations.

*And Elisha prayed, and said, LORD, I pray thee, open his eyes, that he may see. And the LORD opened the eyes of the young man; and he saw: and, behold, the mountain was full of horses and chariots of fire round about Elisha. (2 Kings 6:17)*

The prophetic taps into what is hidden from the natural eyes. It is the ability to see as God sees. If you have a preview of what God has in store for you, there will be no mountain too high for you. You can face any obstacle and have the ability to tackle whatever is standing in your way. The Bible is full of evidence of people like those who were thrown into the fire and were not burned and others who walked on top of the water. They were acting upon a prophetic decree. A prophetic word is enough motivation to cause the impossible to be possible. Prophesy is one of the most re-assuring gifts of all time and is beyond comparison to what the shrinks of this world can offer. Not only must it be desired, Apostle Paul said it must be envied.

The Word of God is precious. It is referred to as "the sure word of prophesy."

*And the child Samuel ministered unto the LORD before Eli. And the word of the LORD was precious in those days; there was no open vision. (1 Samuel 3:1)*

There was a time in the history of Israel when the prophetic word was scarce. Then God raised up a prophet who understood the value of the word of prophesy. He began to open schools of prophesy throughout the region. He raised companies of prophets.

We must be grateful to God that we are not living in such days. We are living in the days of the Holy Ghost and the prophetic grace is being poured out upon all flesh where all shall prophesy. The days of individuals are over. From the first day of the New Testament Church, the Holy Spirit fell upon all the 120 that were present. There were people from all walks of life who witnessed the power of the Holy Ghost when they heard them speak of the great works of God in tongues. "Crete's and Arabians, we do hear them speak in our tongues the wonderful works of God" (Acts 2:11).

## The Prophetic Does Not Discriminate

One good thing about the prophetic is that it does not discriminate against anyone. God allows all people to tap into it. It is designed to cause people to glorify God and ultimately surrender their lives to Him. The prophetic can bring conviction to the hearts of man and lead people to salvation. The Holy Ghost anointing does not require any theological training to qualify His people to be His witnesses as was seen on the day of Pentecost after the resurrection of our Lord Jesus Christ. It was the disciples' encounter with the Holy Ghost that provided sufficient evidence that truly they had an encounter with something supernatural. As a result of that encounter revival broke forth. The Scriptures declare that they all spoke in other tongues, but it was understood by their multi-cultural audience.

The prophetic will always get to its desired impact. God wants to be heard for He is the God of all the families on the earth. He chose a group of people who were hiding in the upper room and, through their encounter with the Holy Spirit, made them known to the world by way of the prophetic. The prophetic can introduce people even when the environment is not conducive for them to be accepted. In this case of the disciples, it was not easy for them to step out in faith because of the fear that was surrounding their allegiance to Jesus. Regardless of the hostility of the environment, this group of believers managed to breakthrough and move in victory even in the midst of their foes. The prophetic can break down every wall of fear and bring to subjection everything that tries to hinder what God is saying. The prophetic breaks all forms of fear and releases people to function with tremendous boldness.

*And when they had prayed, the place was shaken where they were assembled together; and they were all filled with the Holy Ghost, and they spake the word of God with boldness. (Acts 4:31)*

A new movement was born out of the prophetic anointing. When the Holy Ghost came upon them, it released a super natural utterance of prophetic grace. Prophesy is a divine utterance under the influence of the Holy Ghost. The Apostle Paul emphasized we should excel in prophesy. The word "excel" means to super abound in quality and quantity.

## The Prophetic is Key in Spiritual Warfare

The prophetic anointing is a key aspect when it comes to spiritual warfare. The Bible declares,

"Lest Satan should get an advantage of us: for we are not ignorant of his devices" (2 Corinthians 2:11). God has given us the prophetic revelation in order to expose the schemes of our adversary thus enabling us to prepare, advance, and overpower.

Another crucial function of the prophetic is forewarning. There is an incident regarding this very thing when the Apostle Paul was undertaking a trip to Jerusalem. A prophet named Argabus warned him about the dangers that lay ahead of him. However the Apostle Paul continued with his trip, choosing to ignore the warning. It is crucial to note that the prophetic does not dictate to anyone. It is still the person's choice whether to heed the warning or suffer the consequences. The prophetic does not manipulate. Paul continued with his trip and ended up arrested, just as the prophet had forewarned him.

God also uses the prophetic to declare seasons. The Scriptures declare that God does nothing unless He reveals it to His servants, the prophets. These are the days of Elijah prophesied by Malachi 4:5, "Behold, I will send you Elijah the prophet before the coming of the great and dreadful day of the LORD." Malachi declares that before the great and dreadful day comes, God will bring back the spirit of Elijah which represents the prophetic. The same thing applies as Joel was prophesying about the Spirit being poured upon all flesh in the last days. He was speaking about the prophetic. These are prophetic days. Use the prophetic key and it will unlock doors for you.

# Chapter Five

# The Evangelism Key

Evangelism is the proclamation of the good news of the kingdom of God. It is a call to all people to come back to God in repentance, acknowledging their need for salvation and deliverance, which only comes from Him. God often raises up evangelists when His people have backslidden or are living in sin due to the influence of Satan and his fallen angels.

Evangelism or the preaching of the Word dates as far back as the time of Noah. When sin had reached an alarming level and God's judgement was inevitable, God raised up Noah. Biblically known as "the preacher of righteousness," Noah was to call God's people unto repentance and invite them to join him in the ark to avert the judgement which was to come through the flood. This message was to warn the people that unless they repent they would perish. It is never God's intention to punish sinners, but to call them to change their minds and be saved.

However, the people chose not to respond. So

when the consequences occurred, they perished in the flood as God had told Noah. All perished except Noah and his family. The people perished due to their failure to heed the warning that came through the preacher of righteousness. Evangelism is the vehicle through which God brings his message of love to the lost. Through evangelism God offers His people a way out so they do not perish. The scripture declares, "He who believes shall be saved and he who does not will be damned" (see Mark 16:16).

## Evangelism is an Apostolic Assignment

Evangelism is found throughout the Holy Bible. In the Book of Isaiah this important apostolic key is expanded and where we will begin to explore this concept.

*Who hath believed our report? And to whom is the arm of the LORD revealed? (Isaiah 53:1)*

Preaching is an apostolic assignment and a key that opens the kingdom of heaven's doors. The Book of Isaiah is also referred to as the Gospel according to Isaiah or the Book of Salvation. It covers the following aspects:

A. God through judgment would bring Salvation and comfort. Even though God is a God of judgment He desires people to be saved. God first calls man to a place of deliberation before He ultimately passes His judgment on them. Judgement is His last option. If they repent they would be saved; if not they would be judged.

B. The Messiah's salvation will come to all the Nations.

The Prophet Isaiah is considered to be the Old Testament Evangelist as he proclaimed the good news to the exiles as he completes the above verse saying, "And to whom is the arm of the LORD revealed?" What that means is that to everyone who believed the word of the Lord, the arm of the Lord was revealed. For one to believe the Gospel it takes the working of the Holy Spirit to connect him with the message. Then, through believing he will be saved.

In John 6:44 Jesus said, "No man can come to me, except the Father which hath sent me draws him: and I will raise him up at the last day." It is clear that it is God who draws people to His saving grace. There is no salvation that comes without the intervention of God.

It is through evangelism that God invites people into the kingdom and allows them to grow in Him. When evangelism is taking place, God is inviting people to come into a new life. Evangelism is God's hand extended to reach out to them and bring sinners into the Kingdom of God. It is through evangelism that God extends His hand to sinners and invites them to Himself so that He may touch them. The door way to God's eternal kingdom opens wide when one believes His report through the preaching of the Word.

Romans 10:14 clarifies this fact and makes the office of the preacher as important to the believer as rain is to the crop. "How then shall they call on him in whom they have not believed? And how shall they believe in him of whom they have not heard? And how shall they hear without a preacher?" The church at Jerusalem was birthed out of dynamic preaching. The message was very clear; it was a declaration of a new movement which one may call the Jesus culture. Evangelism became the vehicle through which God elaborated on His will to people that were unfamiliar with the Christian movement.

The Word of God is like a mirror and most of the time when God wants His people to be introspective or He wants to give them a warning, He uses evangelism. God often raises men and women from amongst us with revelatory messages that make the intentions of God known. The ways and means of God are not easily understood; neither can they be comprehended with our natural mind. There is a need for someone graced by God to expound on His ways so that our natural minds can understand. Jesus is a perfect example in His use of parables when communicating the mysteries' of heaven.

## Evangelistic Ministry Clarifies Seasons of God

When God is doing a new thing, different interpretations are bound to pop up. This shows the need for an evangelistic ministry to clarify the seasons of

God. In the case of the church in Jerusalem some people began to accuse the movement by associating it with intoxication. There was such a gross misunderstanding that people thought the disciples were drunk, when in fact it was God at work. "Others mocking said, These men are full of new wine" (Acts 2:13).

Let us take note of how this new move came about. After Jesus' resurrection from His gruesome crucifixion and ascended into heaven, a group of about one hundred and twenty of His disciples that were hiding in the upper room began to pray.

In this case one might say evangelism is a revelation ministry that is birthed out of intercession. It is only a prayerful people that have the ability to become preaching people. Evangelism comes out of revelation. It is when God reveals Himself to His servants by His Spirit, demonstrating His saving hand that the captives are set free.

*The Spirit of the Lord GOD is upon me; because the LORD hath anointed me to preach good tidings unto the meek; he hath sent me to bind up the broken hearted, to proclaim liberty to the captives, and the opening of the prison to them that are bound. (Isaiah 61:1)*

Evangelism was birthed from the upper room where the disciples hid and continued in prayer. It ushered in about three thousand souls into the Kingdom of God, signifying that prayer and the infilling of the Holy Spirit precede evangelism.

Peter's evangelism was apologetic, in that it defended the truth. When he stood up to preach, Peter made it clear in his opening statements that none of his colleagues were under the influence of alcohol. Based on the time of the day, it was practically impossible for them to be drunk. He further supported his arguments by quoting the Scriptures from the Book of Joel.

*And it shall come to pass afterward, that I will pour out my spirit upon all flesh; and your sons and your daughters shall prophesy, your old men shall dream dreams, your young men shall see visions. (Joel 2:28)*

Judging from the response of his audience, his preaching carried an anointing that brought great conviction. His preaching enlightened the views of the people and changed their perception. Evangelism will illuminate the spirit and soul, realign the thought patterns, and eliminate the confusion and misunderstanding that often misguides people. Evangelism is an informative key ministry in the kingdom of God. For the kingdom of heaven to expand, it takes this ministry to herald it in a manner that will attract people.

Preaching brings clarity as it announces and highlights the current agenda of God and present day revelation. God's intention is to bring fresh information to His people. He does this by using men and women who are anointed with the power of the Holy Ghost. Evangelism is apostolic and prophetic in nature. Its main call is to defend the faith under the unction of the Holy Spirit. It seeks to communicate the heart of God to man by bringing mankind to conviction and submission to God.

As we see in Acts 2:37, the people responded to the evangelistic message in a very positive way. "Now when they heard this, they were pricked in their heart, and said unto Peter and to the rest of the apostles, Men and brethren, what shall we do?" Hebrews 4:12 explains and supports what happened, "For the word of God is quick, and powerful, and sharper than any two edged sword, piercing even to the dividing asunder of soul and spirit, and of the joints and marrow, and is a discerner of the thoughts and intents of the heart."

Peter's message was so heart piercing, accurate and sincere, that Peter did not sound like he was preaching for the very first time. One would say it was quite impressive because the people responded with such a conviction that they surrendered their lives to the lordship of Jesus. One needs to also bear in mind that Peter was coming from the fishing industry. Being an inexperienced preacher, he managed to make such a tremendous impact his first day on the job that a large number of people were immediately born again. Based on this reflection one would say that it was unique. This was the beginning of his new career; from catching fish to fishing for men.

After Peter's preaching debut, the Scriptures declare that people from all walks of life came and submitted to this new movement. Some sold their houses and farms and became part of this new community of believers. It was not long before this movement became a force to be reckoned with. In no time this movement developed into a mega church with people from all classes of life becoming members.

*And sold their possessions and goods, and parted them to all men, as every man had need. And they, continuing daily with one accord in the temple, and breaking bread from house to house, did eat their meat with gladness and singleness of heart. Praising God, and having favour with all the people. And the Lord added to the church daily such as should be saved. (Acts 2:45-47)*

The Apostle Peter's message empowered people so much that they ended up asking, "What do we do from here?" Peter's immediate response is recorded in Act 2:38. "Then Peter said unto them, 'Repent, and be baptized every one of you in the name of Jesus Christ for the remission of sins, and ye shall receive the gift of the Holy Ghost.' " True evangelistic preaching provides clues and indicates what must be done next. It is in the nature of God that when He wants to communicate His mind to His people He never gives them equations or puzzles. The clear evangelistic preaching of the gospel provides benefits that will be released now and into future generations.

*For the kingdom of God is not meat and drink; but righteousness, and peace, and joy in the Holy Ghost. (Romans 14:17)*

## Evangelism Reaps Benefits Into Future Generations

*And they will be My people, and I will be their God. And I will give them one heart and one way, that they may [reverently] fear Me forever for the good of themselves and of their children after them. And I will make an everlasting covenant with them: I will not turn away from following them to do them good, and I will put My [reverential] fear in their hearts, so that they will not depart from Me. (Jeremiah 32:38-40 AMP)*

When Peter answered their question as to what they should do now that they had heard the truth preached, he elaborated on the blessings that were to follow them. Upon receiving Jesus there was a promise of the Holy Ghost. It could be called, "the kingdom benefit package." This package was to be received and passed on to future generations. God is a God of generations. What He begins with one generation is designed to be passed on to the next. As seen throughout the Bible, God is known as the God of Abraham, Isaac and Jacob.

The Holy Ghost comes to confirm a new life in Christ. Evangelism functions under the unction of the Holy Spirit. It connects people to a life filled with power. However, there are conditions that one must adhere to in order to receive this kingdom benefit package. Repentance comes before baptism. To repent is to totally change one's mind. It is a 180 degree turn when a person says, "I am leaving the old life." Baptism speaks of the outward confession to the world that I am converted and have a new life in Christ. It also serves as a declaration to the entire Body of Christ that one has a new life in Christ. The Holy Spirit is the seal of promise that God gives to those that have received Christ as their personal Lord and Saviour through the preaching of His Word.

In the world we live in today various companies market their products. In most cases they will be targeting the unborn. The advertisements are meant to reach those beyond their current market.

The gospel of our Lord Jesus must be preached throughout the world. It is meant to affect us and well into the future generations. Therefore when Peter preached, he didn't mince his words.

> *Then Peter said unto them, Repent, and be baptized every one of you in the name of Jesus Christ for the remission of sins, and ye shall receive the gift of the Holy Ghost. (Acts 2:38)*

It is for you, your children, your grandchildren, and everyone you come in contact with from now until you pass on into heaven. We have the sure word of prophecy. God spoke it to our forefathers through the prophets, now He is speaking to us through His Son Jesus Christ and the power of the Holy Spirit in our lives.

# Chapter Six

# The Key of Apostolic Teaching

As a minister of the gospel, God has granted me the privilege to travel and bless people through preaching. As I travel to different countries and nations I meet diverse ethnic groups. One of the things I do as a minister of the Word is teach on the practical lessons the Lord has taught me in my walk with Him. I have seen tremendous results as people's lives are changed, transformed, and elevated. I have come to the conclusion that the teaching of the Word of God using practical lessons is absolutely essential. I consider myself privileged as I have seen the practical aspect of my teachings at work in the lives of the people that I minister to. God has always validated what I have taught from His Word. I have seen remarkable results throughout the world confirming how God has changed and elevated people through the ministry of teaching. I am an absolute believer that teaching and how we have applied God's Word in our own lives is a master key given to us by our

Lord Jesus that has the power to produce results.

> *Go ye therefore, and teach all nations, bap-*
> *tizing them in the name of the Father, and*
> *of the Son, and of the Holy Ghost: Teaching*
> *them to observe all things whatsoever I have*
> *commanded you: and, lo, I am with you*
> *always, even unto the end of the world. Amen.*
> *(Matthew 28:19-20)*

## Building a Firm Foundation

> *And they continued steadfastly in the apos-*
> *tles' doctrine and fellowship, and in breaking*
> *of bread, and in prayers. (Acts 2:42)*

One of the fundamental ministries of the church is to provide sound biblical teaching in matters that pertain to faith. This is done to ground and establish God's people in their faith. Therefore, teaching is foundational. Most of the main line churches invest a significant amount of time teaching their new members the foundational doctrines of their denomination. Before new believers are eligible for baptism they must know the basic teachings. Before being considered for full membership they must know what the church stands for. This has been proven strategically important because everything stands or falls based on the condition of the foundation. If the foundation is firm the building will last. Buildings and even nations stand or fall based on the strength of their foundation.

*For which of you, intending to build a tower,
sitteth not down first, and counteth the cost,
whether he have sufficient to finish it? Lest
haply, after he hath laid the foundation, and
is not able to finish it, all that behold it begin
to mock him. (Luke 14:28-29)*

Based on the statement above it is therefore true
that the strength of everything is in the foundation.
Teaching is therefore the only firm foundation in the
life of any believer. There is a common saying that
says, "You are what you are taught." You cannot go
beyond your knowledge; we are all products of the
teachings we have received.

Jesus began His ministry by teaching. He taught
day and night in the synagogues, open air meetings, and in houses; where ever He was given an
opportunity.

*The former treatise have I made, O
Theophilus, of all that Jesus began both to do
and teach. (Acts 1:1)*

Jesus' style of teaching had a demonstrative
aspect to it. Throughout His earthly ministry people
were amazed by His doctrine. He spoke as one with
authority. Hence we see Nicodemus, who even
though he was a teacher himself, came for his share
of teaching. He considered the teaching ministry of
Jesus to be far more superior than his as he confessed
in John 3:2.

*The same came to Jesus by night, and said unto him, Rabbi, we know that thou art a teacher come from God: for no man can do these miracles that thou doest, except God be with him.*

The reason Nicodemus wanted exposure to the teaching ministry of Jesus was two-fold. Jesus demonstrated the power of God and then taught it. He not only taught theory, but had demonstrative proof of what He taught. He came fully displaying the Kingdom of heaven. Jesus was the fullness of the Godhead in bodily form. Teaching is considered to be one of the most fundamental aspects in all religions. Major religions of the world, including Islam and Hinduism, share the common belief that teaching plays an essential role in order to have strong followers. Their main emphasis is to teach their followers to thoroughly establish their belief.

The apostolic teaching in the early New Testament church was part of what made the church grow fast and firm. When apostolic teaching is scarce, stagnation is inevitable. Acts 6:7 clearly indicates what transpires when the Word of God is being taught. "And the word of God increased; and the number of the disciples multiplied in Jerusalem greatly; and a great company of the priests were obedient to the faith." The apostolic church in Jerusalem began to realize a tremendous increase of people joining the faith as a result of the preaching and teaching of the Word. When the Word of God is being taught, growth and multiplication are the immediate results.

Another example is clearly reflected from the words of our Lord Jesus Christ. Before He ascended to heaven, Jesus told His disciples that He was going to send them the Holy Spirit. John 14:26 clearly states the purpose of the coming of the Holy Spirit. "But the Comforter, which is the Holy Ghost, whom the Father will send in my name, he shall teach you all things, and bring all things to your remembrance, whatsoever I have said unto you." They were to continue the teaching ministry of Jesus and the Holy Spirit was to provide sound teaching that would reveal all the aspects and fundamentals of the doctrine of Christ.

Jesus spent most of His time teaching. This was part of His mission. He was sent by the Father to teach. Upon completion of His mission on the earth He said, "But when the Comforter is come, whom I will send unto you from the Father, even the Spirit of truth, which proceedeth from the Father, he shall testify of me." A close observation of the ministry of Jesus confirms that He is indeed the Chief Apostle of our confession. The main definition of the word "apostle" is "a sent one." Similarly, the Holy Spirit carries the "sent one" assignment. Part of the work of the "sent one" is to teach. The teaching that comes from the Holy Spirit carries a revelation of knowledge that unveils what is in the Father's heart to His people. That is why Jesus told His disciples the Holy Spirit would teach them all the truth. When the truth is taught by the Holy Spirit, it produces freedom.

*"Howbeit when he, the Spirit of truth, is come, he will guide you into all truth: for he shall*

*not speak of himself; but whatsoever he shall hear, that shall he speak: and he will shew you things to come." (John 16:13)*

There is need to understand the importance of teaching as the apostolic people of God. Ignorance gives advantage to the enemy. Grounded and growing Christians are the true products of apostolic teaching. The church is therefore founded upon the apostolic doctrine. Acts 2:42 indicates that the apostles taught continuously. "And they continued steadfastly in the apostles' doctrine and fellowship, and in breaking of bread, and in prayers." As a result of their teaching the church expanded in number, strength, and fame. Teaching provides movement, growth, and expansion. It is through teaching that people grow to become powerful because knowledge is power.

## Knowledge is Power—Information Brings Transformation

There was a group of people in the New Testament that tried to stop the church by persecuting it, but it was all in vain. The members of this new church were grounded in the teaching of their faith. A well-taught, well-grounded, well-versed person cannot be easily uprooted. No one should try to fight for or against what they have no knowledge of. Wise words from a seasoned theologian were spoken when a dispute erupted regarding the emergence of the New Testament Jesus movement. People have a tendency to persecute things when they do not understand them, but Gamaliel gave wise counsel in Act 5:38. "And now I say unto you, Refrain from these men, and let them alone: for if this counsel or this work be of men, it will come to nought: But if it be of God, ye cannot overthrow it; lest haply ye be found even to fight against God."

A brief look at the Old Testament church under the leadership of Moses will reveal some of the hardships that he encountered as he led his people under the old covenant.

*And they said unto Moses, Because there were no graves in Egypt, hast thou taken us away to die in the wilderness? Wherefore hast thou dealt thus with us, to carry us forth out of Egypt? (Exodus 14:11)*

One of the reasons for these hardships was the Egyptian indoctrination that these people had been under for so long. Their long stay in Egypt had an effect on their mind-set. They were so deeply entrenched in the ways, culture and religion of Egypt that it became difficult for them to let go of it. By the time Moses arrived to lead them out of Egypt there was a need for a totally new teaching to reshape and realign their thought patterns to a new life in the God of their father Abraham.

Teaching is absolutely necessary if we are to achieve full reformation; information brings transformation. If you want to go places and you desire change, it is important that you begin to acquire new information that is in line with where you want to be. The

Egyptian doctrine had shaped their thought patterns so much that it became difficult for Moses to teach them a new faith. Hence God took Moses out from among the people for forty days and gave him a tailor made teaching in the form of the Ten Commandments. God began this teaching session in Exodus 20:1-3.

*And God spake all these words, saying, I am the LORD thy God, which have brought thee out of the land of Egypt, out of the house of bondage. Thou shalt have no other gods before me.*

The above scripture indicates that God was interested in their transformation. He wanted to bring them out of stagnation and continuous meandering in the bondages they had become accustomed to. The Egyptian indoctrination was the root cause of their stagnation. They were so indoctrinated in slavery that when liberation came they were not ready to embrace it. Teaching must be provided on an on-going basis. It allows people to gradually develop new perspectives which enable them to adjust from the previous anti-God cultural belief systems that enslaved them. Geographical relocation does not necessarily guarantee instant transformation. However, teaching that is provided on an on-going basis can bring about genuine transformation.

*And when the people saw that Moses delayed to come down out of the mount, the people gathered themselves together unto Aaron,*

*and said unto him, Up, make us gods, which*
*shall go before us; for as for this Moses, the*
*man that brought us up out of the land of*
*Egypt, we know not what is become of him.*
*(Exodus 32:1)*

However, Moses discovered it is quite a complicated process to transform a deeply embedded mindset. It takes an apostolic anointing to usher people into new realms of thinking and for them to see the current dealings of God. It takes an apostolic breakthrough doctrine to re-align people to a different mindset. It is not an overnight process; it may take months or even years.

There is also another classic example in the New Testament record of the life of the Apostle Paul. The Apostle Paul's assignment from God was to plant churches among the gentile believers. In the process of obeying that initiative, he encountered challenges similar to Moses. He devoted much of his time teaching in the regions where he planted churches to bring the new converts into new levels of understanding in their new walk of faith. It is through teaching that he shaped strong believers and became one of the greatest leaders of the New Testament church. Just like Moses was given the teachings on the Ten Commandments written by God on the tablets of stone, the Apostle Paul was given the responsibility of writing down the teachings that he received through revelation. His teachings have become part of the New Testament church doctrine that is still relevant, even in the current apostolic reformation. It is interesting to note that his teachings are currently followed throughout the world by all active believers.

## What is an Apostle?

Let us briefly study this word *apostle*. The Greek word for apostle is *apostolos* and was originally a secular term used by the Greeks and the Romans to describe special envoys sent out to establish the dominion of the empire. These envoys were sent to certain territories and charged to subdue, conquer, convert, instruct, train, and establish the new subjects in the culture of the empire.

*And God hath set some in the church, first apostles, secondarily prophets, thirdly teachers, after that miracles, then gifts of healings, helps, governments, diversities of tongues. (1 Corinthians 12:28)*

The apostle is first and foremost a pioneer. The Greek word for pioneer, "proton" means "first in time, order, or rank." "First in time" describes the pioneer. Apostles are able to pioneer new truths and revelations and bring them into new territories. Pioneers have the ability to advance ahead of others and to instil greater confidence into the hearts of the rest of the Body of Christ who lag behind. Their forward advancement opens up new doors for the effective ministry of the church. Their ministry provides the cutting edge to influence and to impact society.

One might call it apostolic teaching. Apostolic

teaching is the key that establishes every believer who confesses Jesus as Lord and Saviour. It irons out all misconceptions and roots out every doctrine of devils. It highlights the key fundamental aspects of faith in Christ Jesus our Lord. The Apostle Paul went about teaching in different places and sometimes had to stay as long as three years in one location.

*Therefore watch, and remember that by the space of three years I ceased not to warn every one night and day with tears.* (Acts 20:31)

It takes more than one sermon to change people's ideologies and theologies. It is rather an ongoing prophetic and apostolic revelation of cutting edge breakthrough anointing that brings people to a place of maturity. In the case of Moses in the Old Testament church, it took a generation. After ministering for a period of forty years he managed to get through to only two people who became the only successful graduates. The rest of the people died in the wilderness. They did not see the Promise Land because they were not completely transformed by Moses' teaching. It was the next generation under the leadership of Joshua that managed to transition and cross over to inherit the Promise Land.

*And they brought up an evil report of the land which they had searched unto the children of Israel, saying, The land, through which we have gone to search it, is a land that eateth up the inhabitants thereof; and all the people that we saw in it are men of a great stature. (Numbers 13:32)*

*And Caleb stilled the people before Moses, and said, Let us go up at once, and possess it; for we are well able to overcome it. (Numbers 13:30)*

## Apostolic and Prophetic Wisdom

*Therefore also said the wisdom of God, I will send them prophets and apostles, and some of them they shall slay and persecute.* (Luke 11:49)

The wisdom of God speaks of strategy. God sends wisdom. It is through this wisdom that the enemy is defeated. In the frontline of God's army lies apostolic and prophetic wisdom that causes the people of God to advance with confidence and boldness. New joy is realized through the grace that comes by the wisdom of God. Ignorance causes people to persecute prophets even to the extent of eliminating them. Those that persecute the prophets do that to their own peril. It is a common thing throughout history that prophets were martyred. Prophets teach under a tremendous anointing of God's wisdom as confirmed in the above passage. Their teaching releases wisdom.

*And after that he gave unto them judges about the space of four hundred and fifty years, until Samuel the prophet. (Acts 13:20)*

*What shall I more say? For the time would fail me to tell of Gideon, and of Barak,*

> *and of Samson, and of Jephthae; of David
> also, and Samuel, and of the prophets.
> (Hebrews 11:32)*

Jesus taught on an ongoing basis. He gave His apostolic gift of teaching to some of His disciples and He continues to teach through this gift to the Body of Christ still today. The ministry of teaching finds its origin in the Old Testament. The Old Testament Prophet Samuel is considered to be a teaching prophet who established prophetic colleges. Prophets carry a teaching grace that empowers the community of believers.

Samuel was the last of the judges and first of the line of prophets and kings. Moses was the original example of a prophet and Jesus was to be modelled on Moses' prophetic role. Thus from Samuel to Malachi we have the ministry of the Major and Minor Prophets. It seems evident from the Scriptures that Samuel, under the direction of the Lord, gathered young men who were hungry for the things of God into schools of the prophets. Here they received education and instruction out of the Law of Moses and were taught how to respond to the Spirit of the Lord in worship and prophecy.

> *And as for thine asses that were lost three
> days ago, set not thy mind on them; for they
> are found. And on whom is all the desire of
> Israel? Is it not on thee, and on all thy father's
> house? (1 Samuel 9:20)*

The Scriptures speak of these centers as where the "sons of the prophets" would gather together in preparation for ministry. The list of cities below came to be known as centers for training the "sons of the prophets."

- Ramah 1 Samuel 19:18-24
- Bethel 2 Kings 2:10
- Jericho 2 Kings 2:5,7,15
- Gilgal 2 Kings 4:38, 2:1

The dominant purpose in the establishment of these "Schools of the Prophets" was to maintain the spirit of the law. If Moses stood for the letter of the law, the prophets indeed stood for the spirit of the Law. The true prophets of God never contradicted the letter of the law, they upheld it. But when the law degenerated into a dead form and became mere ritual, the Holy Spirit came upon the prophets to inspire and revive the spirit of the law. Thus we have the major and minor prophets who imparted God's wisdom and law. Then there were four hundred silent years until John the Baptist came on the scene as recorded in Luke 7:26-28.

"The 'Sons of the Prophets' were responsible for teaching the Word of God, and making sure that the people of God stayed on course; one may say they were defenders of the truth" (Kevin Conner).

God is raising a generation that will teach His Word in every sphere of life. This generation will not be limited by the four corners of the church. They will be found standing and declaring the Word of the

Lord in the highways and bi-ways. Not only where we gather, but also where we scatter. They will be found in the market place, in the political world, in the entertainment world, and in the communities where they live. This generation will teach this by demonstrating a lifestyle developed through apostolic teaching. The Apostle Paul refers to these generations as epistles not written by human hands in 2 Corinthians 3:2-3.

*Ye are our epistle written in our hearts, known and read of all men: Forasmuch as ye are manifestly declared to be the epistle of Christ ministered by us, written not with ink, but with the Spirit of the living God; not in tables of stone, but in fleshy tables of the heart.*

Just as the sons of the prophets were responsible for defending the truth, apostolic churches will become centers of apostolic teachings that will groom and raise new Sons of the Prophets who will be champions of the Scriptures. In the New Testament there was a man raised by God whose name was Apollos. He is a typical example of what I'm referring to.

*And a certain Jew named Apollos, born at Alexandria, an eloquent man, and mighty in the Scriptures, came to Ephesus. (Acts 18:24)*

He is referred to as the "champion of Scriptures." We also find another group of people similar to

Apollos in the city of Beria. This group was known as "students of the Word." They did not take anything for granted but always compared line upon line, precept upon precept what was being taught. They were always willing to verify using the Word of the Lord to validate what was being taught.

> *These were more noble than those in Thessalonica, in that they received the word with all readiness of mind, and searched the Scriptures daily, whether those things were so. (Acts 17:11)*

Paul encouraged his spiritual son Timothy, who was part of his apostolic team, to carefully study the Word of God. "Study to shew thyself approved unto God, a workman that needeth not to be ashamed, rightly dividing the word of truth" (2 Timothy 2:15).

I believe that apostolic teaching is the key to unlocking stability and growth in the church. The greatest things in life will happen when people spend more time in the apostolic teachings. The New Testament church was full of action because the leadership was sold out to a life of teaching. Miracles happened in the streets and everywhere they went due to the fact that there was an apostolic center that was responsible for teaching and stirring up the Spirit of miracles.

The Apostle Peter was one of the disciples of our Lord Jesus Christ who saw Jesus first hand. Yet he was limited in his understanding until he had an encounter with God through a vision where he was taught not to discriminate. After the vision, he was given an opportunity to go into a new are of his teaching ministry. He felt he was inadequate to minister to those outside the Jewish community due to his limited knowledge of God, but this personal vision caused him to confess something radically new.

*Then Peter opened his mouth, and said, of a truth I perceive that God is no respecter of persons. (Acts 10:34)*

Peter's words were referring to this new knowledge. He said, "Now I know." Knowledge eliminates prejudice, brings freedom, and releases Godly wisdom. In the Book of Acts, the apostolic leadership took a solid stand when they said they didn't want to involve themselves with the distribution of food, but to continue with teaching and prayer. As servants of God, they needed to focus on what they were called to do using the gifts God had placed within them.

In 2 Timothy 2:24 Paul says when the man of God focuses on teaching strife will be eliminated. "And the servant of the Lord must not strive; but be gentle unto all men, apt to teach, patient. . . ." The knowledge that comes from the Scriptures brings the man of God into that state of productivity.

# Chapter Seven

# The Giving Key

I remember an incident that happened when I went to minister in the Kingdom of Swaziland, Africa. A friend had asked me to conduct a series of meetings, some of which were going to take place during lunchtime in the town center. People who were employed around that area came to spend an hour in prayer and to hear the Word of God. As I continued to minister during that week, the Lord gave me a specific Word of Knowledge that I was to collect an offering and special prayer requests. I was a bit skeptical at first, as I did not want to sound like I just wanted to collect an offering. As a visiting preacher I did not want it to sound like I was merchandising the gospel. Little did I know that God had a lesson attached to this instruction that I only discovered at the end of that day. I learned that God wanted to teach me a principle that was found in the power of giving.

I did as God had instructed me and requested people to write their special prayers on pieces of paper and turn them in with their offerings. A certain lady was delayed in coming to the lunch meeting and could not submit her special prayer request and offering. She followed me to my hotel and when she caught up with me, gave me her offering and request as she believed God for a miracle. As she handed me the offering, the Lord gave me a word for her that this same time next year, she was going to have a child. She was shocked with the news and confessed just how reckless she had been living her life. She had been drinking and smoking and could not understand how God would want to do such a thing for her considering her relationship with Him. I responded by saying to her I was just a messenger of God and that is what the Lord was saying. I lead her in the sinner's prayer and she accepted the Lord as her Savior.

After three months I returned to Swaziland, the same lady came to the meeting and asked me if I remembered her. I told her I did not, but she reminded me that she was the one I told that God said she was going to have a baby.

Well, I became a bit religious about it and said, "Praise God, let us continue to believe God."

She said to me, "No, Pastor look at me properly."

I took a closer look at her as she had asked and discovered that her belly had grown. She told me she was three months pregnant. We all got very excited and the next year when I returned to Swaziland, she came and presented the child to me. I dedicated the child to the Lord. She then gave me a full testimony of her miracle. She had been unable to give birth because as a child she had undergone an operation which had damaged her fallopian tubes. The gynecologist had told her it would be impossible for her to give birth. At the time when I had told her the Word from God, she had gone and told her husband and mother, who because of the doctor's report, had concluded she had met a liar and a false prophet.

When the word came to pass they were so afraid to see me, they apologized to her and said, "Truly, this is a man of God."

The lesson I learned was that the power of giving had released the blessing of the baby. To be more precise, she gave a gift of seven dollars and that's all it took to see this special miracle. I have had many testimonies after that of people who gave to my ministry either directly or indirectly and God supernaturally gave them a great harvest.

## The Legacy of Giving

*Then Peter began to say unto him, Lo, we have left all, and have followed thee. And Jesus answered and said, Verily I say unto you, There is no man that hath left house, or brethren, or sisters, or father, or mother, or wife, or children, or lands, for my sake, and the gospel's, but he shall receive an hundredfold now in this time, houses, and brethren, and sisters, and mothers, and children, and lands, with persecutions; and in the world to come eternal life. (Mark 10:28-30)*

It is worth noting that there is a great legacy

attached to giving which entails rewards in both realms; in this world and that which is to come. Our eternal rewards are directly linked to how we perform our earthly duties. As we read in Mark 10:28-30, there is a powerful revelation from God's Word that when we pray wisely our inheritance will be great. All forms of giving must be linked with prayer. Therefore it becomes imperative for us to pray before giving so that our giving becomes God directed.

*And he left the oxen, and ran after Elijah, and said, Let me, I pray thee, kiss my father and my mother, and then I will follow thee. And he said unto him, Go back again: for what have I done to thee? (1 Kings 19:20)*

It is also important to pray before we embark on any major decision, journey, career, or marriage. Great men and women throughout the Bible did nothing without properly consulting God in prayer. When giving, it is paramount that we pray so that our giving is in line with the will of God. In Acts 10:4 we find an interesting occurrence. "And when he looked on him, he was afraid, and said, What is it, Lord? And he said unto him, Thy prayers and thine alms are come up for a memorial before God." Our giving is recorded in heaven. The angel of the Lord communicated with Cornelius and unveiled the mystery of what his prayers and giving had been doing behind the scenes. One would say it had reached record level and had become a memorial before the throne of God, so much so that the heavens acknowledged it. Giving pleases God and releases the blessings of God. A close study of the men and women of God who walked on earth before us, shows that giving was a key ingredient that connected them with the favor of heaven and released the abundance of blessings showered upon them in unprecedented measure.

In contrast, when we study the account of Cain and Abel, we come to discover that death of the first martyr in the Bible was directly linked to his giving lifestyle. Abel was murdered by his brother Cain because he had given a gift that God was well pleased with. On the other hand Cain had given a gift that God would not accept. This story teaches us that not all giving pleases God. Therefore, when we give we should always start by doing an introspection of the condition of our hearts concerning what we are about to give. It is not the quantity but the quality of our giving that moves heavens.

*And Abel, he also brought of the firstlings of his flock and of the fat thereof. And the LORD had respect unto Abel and to his offering. (Genesis 4:4)*

Abel's giving was sincere and in line with what God wanted. As such, after his death his blood spoke before God and he was vindicated.

Genesis 22:17 shows us giving carries a perpetual blessing that will benefit even future generations.

*That in blessing I will bless thee, and in multiplying I will multiply thy seed as the stars of the heaven, and as the sand which is upon the sea shore; and thy seed shall possess the gate of his enemies.*

Abraham gave freely and he became a friend of God. It is quite interesting to note that God gave him a test in the area of giving. God asked Abraham to offer his only son (Genesis 22). Abraham was unselfish and more than willing to carry out the test. Therefore, God was not ashamed to call Abraham His friend.

Giving opens heaven's doors and brings upon us heaven's unlimited supply. As recorded in Malachi 3:10, when giving takes place the windows of heaven are commanded to open and release blessings that one cannot contain. "Bring ye all the tithes into the storehouse, that there may be meat in mine house, and prove me now herewith, saith the LORD of hosts, if I will not open you the windows of heaven, and pour you out a blessing, that there shall not be room enough to receive it."

The New Testament gospel would be somehow incomplete if the giving aspect of ministry had been avoided. The entire message of the Book of Acts is interwoven with the giving aspect. The social outreach to the needy, the healing of the diseased, and the salvation of the human soul must all be considered as part and parcel of the giving ministry of the church. The Apostles gave themselves to teach, to love, and to care for the people. That is the reason I have emphasised giving as an apostolic key. People who got saved in the early church gave either their money or their land, gave their gifts and talents, and gave their intellectual properties. I call that apostolic giving, and that giving opened up the entire region for the preaching of the gospel.

The Apostle Paul said in Philippians 4:19, "But my God shall supply all your need according to his riches in glory by Christ Jesus." This statement was motivated by the fact that the people he was addressing were situated in a very poor region that naturally made it difficult for them to give. However, against the odds they collected an offering that impacted Paul's heart. In return he mentioned it with gratitude and the full realization that it was a sacrifice that they had made. We must realize though, that the reason for the blessings of God in their lives was due to their partnership with him in ministry. Apostolic partnership releases apostolic blessings. In Philippians 4:19, Paul was decreeing that all their needs be met with the glorious blessings of heaven because of their generous giving and partnering with him in ministry.

Many believers today confess Paul's statement out of context. They use his word as a confession of prosperity without understanding why and to whom it was said. That scripture must be viewed in this light. Paul was giving a vote of thanks to the people who had partnered with his apostolic assignment. Partnership with apostolic workers will release God's glorious supply and God often rewards those that partner with His servants. Our giving must be apostolic, meaning it must be for the purpose of sending the Word of God to its desired destiny. Giving is designed to advance the work of the ministry. Giving to those that are of the household of faith brings you into partnership with their divine assignment. In turn, this giving releases blessings to the extent that all of our needs are met.

This is seen in the example of the Old Testament story of the widow during the Prophet Elijah's time (1 Kings 17:7-24). The people of faith who perceived God's servants as representatives of heaven received glorious blessings beyond their expectations. The story of a widow in Elijah's time who had one last meal for her and her child to eat before they would most likely starve to death, illustrates that. She gave the last she had to the prophet and God in return supernaturally sustained her life and that of her child. Her giving to the man of God released a flow of food for her and her child until the drought broke. Her life was literally saved from starvation because of her giving.

In Acts 9:36-40 we read of Tabitha who ministered to the widows in need. When she died the widows prayed and she was resurrected back to life because of her works of charity. At this juncture allow me to say that giving has the power of a second chance. The story of Lazarus can be summed up as the story of a family that had a partnership with Jesus. During the days of Jesus' ministry on earth, He often hung out with Lazarus and his family. When Lazarus died Jesus said, "This death is for the glory of God." Due to the giving of Lazarus and his family, Jesus came and resurrected him from the dead, even though Lazarus had been dead for three days (John 11:11).

Giving has the power to give life to that which was dead. Are things dying around you, are your finances slowly dying, is your family surrounded with the spirit of death? Find an apostolic worker and give with an expectation to see the glory of God released in your life.

## God Transfers Wealth into the Hands of His Children

One day I was led to go and give to one of the apostolic workers in our city. I gave him a specific amount of money as seed for his ministry. On my way back home I received a phone call from someone else notifying me that he had just paid a huge sum of money into my bank account. The rest of that week I had similar phone calls from different people who were putting money into my account. It was one of the most glorious weeks I ever had, full of blessing and overflow. The glories of giving are still available to us today; the windows of heaven will be opened until we have no room left in which to put the blessings of God.

When studying the Scriptures closely, we will see how God prospered His people by transferring the wealth of other nations into the hands of His children. There were three major transfers of wealth in the Old Testament.

1) The first was when God put the entire wealth of Egypt in the hands of Joseph, a Hebrew boy who had been sold into slavery by his

brothers. God elevated Joseph to a prominent position where he was in charge of the wealth of Egypt. This was a fulfilment of the promise of God that had been given to his great grandfather Abraham who was a great giver. He gave at every opportunity and future generations began to reap the rewards of his giving lifestyle.

2) The second was when the children of Israel were living in Egypt and God spoke to Moses saying that they were to ask their neighbours for jewelry as they needed it for worship where they were heading to. They left Egypt with great wealth. Egypt is symbolic of the world of non-believers of which every child of God was once part. When God brought us out He wanted to demonstrate Himself to us just as He did through the children of Israel under Moses. One of the conditions of the Exodus was that they did not leave Egypt empty handed; they got favor and received from their neighbors a great amount of jewelry (Exodus 12:33-36).

I'm of the belief that when God brought us out "the world" He wanted us to have more than enough so that we could become the modern financiers of the gospel with the wealth that is in the world. I maintain that the church must be wealthy in order for it to reach out to the lost. However, the church must be a giving church in order for us to receive. Giving and receiving work hand in hand.

3) The third major transfer of wealth was when God ordered Moses to build the tabernacle in the wilderness. The Scriptures declare that people gave until there was more than enough for the purpose of building the house of God (Exodus 36:6-7). God raises willing partners who will stop at nothing to further the kingdom of God. There is a transfer of wealth that is coming upon the apostolic people of God so that they can continue to pronounce the kingdom message without the hiccups of financial lack.

# Final Word

# Be Fishers of Men

God's promise to give us the nations is recorded in Psalm 2:8, "Ask of me, and I shall give thee the heathen for thine inheritance, and the uttermost parts of the earth for thy possession." God wants us to be fishers of men in order for Him to harvest souls. He depends on our prayers and our giving. God's heart beat is to see the whole human race saved. He demonstrated that by giving us His Son. He revealed that when we ask Him for souls, not only will He respond by giving us those souls to be converted into His kingdom but that ultimately these souls will become our heritage. Every time we partner with God to seek after lost souls, He rewards us with an inheritance that no one can measure or describe.

Unless we tap into these keys our countries will be under evangelized, our regions and the nations of the world will not see the glorious gospel of the kingdom of God. It is about time we put the key of giving, the key of praying, the key of waiting, the key of prophecy, the key of unity, the key of teaching, and the key of evangelism at work and see this world becoming the kingdom of our God. The whole world is waiting for the manifestation of the sons of God. You and I have the keys; the sure keys of David, whatever we bind on earth shall be bound in heaven.

> *And I tell you, you are Peter [Greek, Petros—a large piece of rock], and on this rock I will build My church, and the gates of Hades (the powers of the infernal region) shall not overpower it [or be strong to its detriment or hold out against it]. I will give you the keys of the kingdom of heaven; and whatever you bind (declare to be improper and unlawful) on earth must be what is already bound in heaven; and whatever you loose (declare lawful) on earth must be what is already loosed in heaven. (Matthew 16:19 AMP)*

> *And the key of the house of David will I lay upon his shoulder; so he shall open, and none shall shut; and he shall shut, and none shall open. And I will fasten him as a sure nail in a sure place. (Isaiah 22:22)*

For ministry information
Please contact:

**Wells of Life Churches International**
PO Box 1805
Port Elizabeth
6001

RSA
Tel: (+27) 041 582 4100

Email: wellsoflife1@gmail.com
www.alidimpateyaministries.org and www.wellsof-
lifechurchesint.com

CPSIA information can be obtained at www.ICGtesting.com
Printed in the USA
BVOW040955260912

301389BV00004B/1/P

9 781619 969254